Clues to Culture

Clues to Culture

A CROSS-CULTURAL READING/WRITING BOOK

Pamela Hartmann

EVANS COMMUNITY ADULT SCHOOL
LOS ANGELES UNIFIED SCHOOL DISTRICT

RANDOM HOUSE  NEW YORK

THIS IS AN BOOK

9 8 7 6 5 4 3 2 1

Library of Congress Cataloging-in-Publication Data

Hartmann, Pamela.
   Clues to culture : a cross-cultural reading/writing book / Pamela
Hartmann.
     p.   cm.
  Includes index.
  ISBN 0-394-38272-2
  1. College readers. 2. English language—Rhetoric. 3. English
language—Textbooks for foreign speakers.   I. Title.
PE1417.H283 1989
808′.0427—dc19   88-28178
                                         CIP

Manufactured in the United States of America
Sponsoring editor: Eirik Børve
Developmental editor: Mary McVey Gill
Senior production manager: Karen Judd
Production supervisor: Renée Reeves
Project editor: Marie Deer
Copyeditor: Patricia Campbell
Art director: Jamie Sue Brooks
Cover and text designer: Rick Chafian
Cover artist: Valerie Winemiller
Illustrators: Roni Shepherd, Valerie Winemiller
Typesetter: Interactive Composition Corporation
Printer and binder: Malloy Lithographing, Inc.

Contents

Chapter 4   At the Table   43

READING SKILLS: Guessing meaning from context: using details around a
word; using information after a colon
WRITING SKILLS: Using *when, while, as, after, before,* and *if*

Chapter 5   *Yes or No?*   57

READING SKILLS: Understanding a word from information that occurred
before it; Understanding meaning when words are left out
WRITING SKILLS: Using *however, therefore, in addition,* and *then*

Chapter 6   Suggestions and Invitations   71

READING SKILLS: Recognizing invitations and suggestions;
Understanding the use of italics
WRITING SKILLS: Avoiding and repairing fragments; Writing paragraphs
(introduction)

Chapter 7   Criticism   87

READING SKILLS: Understanding requests or commands with infinitives;
Understanding sarcasm
WRITING SKILLS: Avoiding and repairing run-on sentences;
Understanding paragraph form (review)

Chapter 8 Family Life 101

READING SKILLS: Understanding infinitives that show purpose;
Distinguishing fact from opinion
WRITING SKILLS: Using adjective clauses (1); Writing paragraphs:
supporting material (reasons)

Chapter 9 Work 117

READING SKILLS: Understanding the use of quotation marks;
Understanding indirect speech
WRITING SKILLS: Using adjective clauses (2); Writing paragraphs:
supporting material (examples)

Chapter 10 Education 133

READING SKILLS: Identifying the agent in the passive voice;
Understanding newspaper headlines
WRITING SKILLS: Using adjective clauses (review); Writing paragraphs:
supporting material (contrast)

Preface

OVERVIEW / PURPOSE

Clues to Culture is an intermediate-level reading/writing text intended primarily for adult students of ESL (English as a second language) in both academic and adult education programs. The text presents reading and writing skills essential to academic success and everyday life as well as an abundance of information on the customs and beliefs in North American culture. In a sense, it offers an "inside look" at how Americans think.

This book may be used either as a supplement in a general ESL class or as a core text in a class that emphasizes reading and writing or culture. It is coordinated with *ETC 4: Culture and Communication* in grammatical sequence but can be used independently.

The purpose of *Clues to Culture* is threefold: (1) to give students stimulating readings and to teach strategies for understanding them; (2) to teach writing skills that enable students to construct grammatical sentences and well-organized paragraphs; and (3) to present an explanation of behavior and attitudes considered appropriate in North American culture.

Each chapter focuses on a cultural point or theme, such as eating customs, family life, attitudes toward work, and concepts of time. The solution to the mystery story in each chapter hinges on this cultural point; once students understand the custom, behavior, or attitude (explained in the nonfiction reading in each chapter), they will be able to figure out "who done it."

THE READING SKILLS

The reading selections are fun and easy enough to encourage students to read more, yet challenging enough to require them to "reach." Each chapter includes a brief explanation of specific reading skills and exercises to practice them. The reading selections become progressively longer and more difficult as students acquire skills and vocabulary. It should be noted that vocabulary items presented in one chapter are recycled in subsequent chapters to allow for a rapid increase in vocabulary.

THE WRITING SKILLS

Writing skills are presented in Part 4 of each chapter. Students first practice the targeted skill (such as the use of basic punctuation, conjunctions, or adjective clauses) by either combining sentences or "repairing" incorrect sentences. They then use this skill to write original sentences based on the theme of the chapter. In addition, the second half of the text introduces students to paragraph organization and guides them, step by step, toward expressing their own ideas in paragraph form.

CHAPTER ORGANIZATION

Each chapter consists of four parts. The first two parts contain fiction readings (Parts 1 and 2 of a mystery story) and exercises based on the reading skills covered in that chapter. Part 3 contains a nonfiction reading and discussion questions on the chapter theme. Part 4 focuses on writing skills.

Part 1

Picture Clues: a prereading exercise consisting of a picture and true/false questions about it; this section sets the tone for the chapter and encourages students to make predictions before reading

Fiction Reading, Part 1: the first half of a mystery story; a controlled reading selection on the theme of the chapter; the detectives introduced in this section of the first chapter are encountered throughout the book

Did You Understand the Story? a postreading exercise to help students check their general comprehension of the selection

Reading Clues: specific suggestions, followed by exercises, to help students guess meaning from context and understand details

Part 2

Picture Clues: a prereading exercise, similar to that in Part 1, that introduces the second half of the mystery story

Fiction Reading, Part 2: the conclusion of the mystery story; the solution ("who done it?") is missing from this conclusion, and students will be led to figure it out in subsequent exercises

Did You Understand the Story?   comprehension questions about Part 2 of the story

Can You Figure It Out?   comprehension questions that focus on the cultural point of the chapter and bring students closer to the solution of the mystery

Reading Clues: more practice based on the explanations in Part 1

Part 3

Nonfiction Reading: a reading selection explaining the cultural point of the chapter

Can You Solve the Mystery?   questions that incorporate information from the nonfiction reading and lead to the solution of the mystery

Discussing Culture: cross-cultural questions that relate the readings to the students' lives and stimulate discussion

Part 4

Guidelines for Writing Sentences: an explanation, followed by exercises, covering such topics as the use of conjunctions and adjective clauses and how to correct run-on sentences

Guidelines for Writing Paragraphs (Chapters 6–10):   an explanation and example of paragraph organization, followed by a list of suggested topics; students choose a topic and write an original paragraph, based on the cross-cultural theme of the chapter

TEACHING SUGGESTIONS

Part 1

Picture Clues: The skill of anticipation—forming predictions about what is to be read—is an important part of active reading. The pictures and true/false exercises are designed to encourage students to anticipate. After asking students to do the items in the *Picture Clues* section, you might ask the class a few additional questions: What does the woman look like? What else can you guess about the man? What do you think will happen in the story?

Initial Reading: Ask students to read Part 1 of the story silently, since this is the most common form of reading; or read the selection aloud while students follow along silently. The latter technique has two advantages: (1) students can hear your intonation, and (2) students who normally read slowly and word/by/word/like/this/ will be encouraged to read in phrases, moving their eyes across the page smoothly and quickly. Regardless of the method you use, you should encourage students to read quickly, *without a dictionary.* Emphasize the importance of guessing the meanings of new words and of simply getting the main idea.

Did You Understand the Story?   Students should answer these questions quickly, without looking back at the reading selection. The answers can be checked later, after students reread the selection.

Reading Clues: This section varies from chapter to chapter; it guides students toward understanding new words by using the context in which the words are found. After a few chapters, students will begin to see that it is often possible to understand a new word without touching a dictionary. It's a good idea to reinforce this skill elsewhere in the class—e.g., when students encounter a new word on a grammar practice handout.

Rereading: Students reread the selection, this time more carefully, focusing on details. This reading should be done silently. Again, encourage the students to apply the skill of guessing meaning from context. When they finish rereading the selection, they should check their initial answers in the section called *Did You Understand the Story?*

Part 2

The same suggestions for exercises from Part 1 apply here. When students finish the initial reading and exercises, ask them to read the selection again silently.

Part 3

To prepare students for the nonfiction reading selection, you might ask the class a few prereading questions to set the tone for the topic. These should be fairly general—e.g., Do people in the United States or Canada greet each other differently from the way people greet each other in your country? (Chapter 1) *or* How is family life in the United States or Canada different from your country? (Chapter 8). Have the students read the selection silently; or read it aloud as they follow along silently.

Can You Solve the Mystery?   Ask students to turn back to Part 2 of the mystery and apply the information from Part 3 as they answer these questions. The questions should lead them to the solution of the mystery.

Discussing Culture: Encourage students to actively practice their newly learned vocabulary words as they express their opinions and share ideas in answering the questions in this section. These questions may be answered in various ways. For example:

1. Ask the questions of the entire class. The advantage of this technique is that the teacher can control the discussion and encourage students to expand on their ideas. Also, students have the opportunity to hear the opinions of many others. The disadvantage, though, is that few students may volunteer to speak.

2. Have students discuss the answers in small groups of three to four people. A representative from each group can then report the group's ideas to the whole class.

3. Have students discuss the answers with just one partner. This technique will encourage the participation of students who are usually too shy to speak in a larger group.

Part 4

Read through the boxed explanation with your students to make sure they understand it. You might put a few additional examples on the board. Have students work individually on the controlled exercises on punctuation (Chapter 1) and sentence combining or sentence correction (other chapters).

For those chapters with a section in which students write original sentences, you may want to "prime the pump" by adding an example of your own to that in the book—or by asking a few students to volunteer examples and write them on the board.

For those chapters with a section on paragraph organization, read through the explanation and example with the students and make sure that they understand them. Give the students a few minutes to choose a topic and write a topic sentence for their own paragraphs. It is a good idea to check each student's topic sentence quickly before he or she continues with the paragraph. If, after correcting the finished paragraphs, you don't feel that the class has mastered the skill, assign another paragraph—based on a different topic from the list—as homework.

ACKNOWLEDGMENTS

Much appreciation goes to Elaine Kirn, whose idea this book was initially; to Mary McVey Gill, for her time, patience, and editing; to Florene Rozen, JoAnne Shayne, and Andrew Morris-Machai, for help with research; to Roni Shepherd and Valerie Winemiller, for bringing the stories to life with their drawings; and to Marie Deer, project editor, for making everything go smoothly.

P. H.

1 Greetings

READING SKILLS:

Guessing meaning from context: using pictures, information after a dash, and information after *that is* and *in other words*

WRITING SKILLS:

Using capitalization, periods, and quotation marks

Part 1: Fiction Reading

A. Picture clues. Pictures can help us understand a story. They give us *clues* (pieces of information). What do you think happens in Part 1 of the story? Before you read the story, look for clues in the pictures on this page. Then write T (true) or F (false) on the lines.

———— 1. A short, bald man comes to a detective agency.

———— 2. Probably one of the detectives is a woman.

———— 3. Bob Brass is a car salesman.

———— 4. Someone is stealing money.

———— 5. There is a crime at a bank.

B. Read the story. Try to guess the meaning of the new words. Don't use a dictionary.

The Case of the Stolen Fashion Designs

Sharon Holmes—a famous detective—was sitting in her office one morning when a short, bald man walked in.

She greeted him and introduced herself.

"Hello, Ms. Holmes, I'm Bob Brass," the man said as he shook hands with Sharon. "I need your help."

"Please sit down and tell me your problem, Mr. Brass," Sharon said.

Bob Brass looked miserable; in other words, he appeared to be tired, tense, and unhappy. There were dark circles under his eyes, and his hands were shaking.

"I'm a fashion designer," he said. "That is, I think of ideas for new styles of clothing and describe them to my artists. The artists draw pictures of my designs. Then other people make the outfits—the dresses or suits."

"Your designs are famous, Mr. Brass!" Sharon said. "I often see your outfits in stores. They're wonderful!"

Bob Brass smiled. "Well, if you can find the thief who is stealing my designs, I'll give you any outfit you want from my factory. And please call me Bob."

"All right, Bob. Tell me about the thief," Sharon said.

"I'm afraid that it's one of my employees—someone who works in my office or factory. This spy—the man or woman who is stealing my secrets—is working for a clothing company in the country of Xenrovia," Bob Brass said. "The thief is taking my designs before I can put them into the stores. Then he, or she, gives them to the Xenrovian company, and they make the outfits. They use cheap material and sew too quickly, so the quality of the outfits is very poor. This company is selling my designs all over the world, and I'm losing money fast. If you can't find this spy, I'll soon be bankrupt; that is, I'll be so poor that I'll have to go out of business."

. . . To be continued

C. Did you understand the story? Answer these questions about it.

1. What kind of work does Sharon Holmes do?
2. Who was Bob Brass? Why was he worried about his business?
3. Who did Bob Brass think the thief was?
4. In your opinion, how will Sharon try to find the spy from the Xenrovian company?

READING CLUE

You don't always need to use a dictionary for a new word. Sometimes you can guess the meaning. Pictures often help you guess the meanings of new words.

Example: Sharon Holmes was sitting in her office one morning when a short, *bald* man walked in.

Look at picture 1. What does *bald* mean?

a. handsome   c. happy
b. with no hair   d. very, very old

The picture tells you that *bald* means "with no hair."

D.   Choose the correct definition of each underlined word. Use the pictures.

1. She greeted him and introduced herself. (Picture 1)
   a. hugged   c. welcomed; met in a certain way
   b. looked at   d. kissed
2. He appeared to be tired, tense, and unhappy. (Picture 1)
   a. nervous   c. calm
   b. hot   d. hungry
3. The thief is taking my designs before I can put them into the stores. (Picture 2)
   a. clothing plans   c. suits and dresses
   b. hats and coats   d. secrets

READING CLUE

Sometimes the words after a dash (—) or between dashes give more information about the word or phrase before the dash. Often, this information is the definition of a new word.

Example: Sharon Holmes—a famous detective—was sitting in her office one morning. (The words between dashes explain that Sharon Holmes is a famous detective.)

E.   Find phrases after or between dashes in Part 1 of the story. Use the information to answer these questions.

1. What's an outfit?
2. What's an employee?
3. What's a spy?

READING CLUE

A sentence after the phrase *that is* or *in other words* can explain the word or phrase before it.

Example: I'm a fashion designer; that is, I think of ideas for new styles of clothing and describe them to my artists. (The words after *that is* explain that a fashion designer is a person who thinks of ideas for new styles of clothing.)

F.   Explain the underlined words in these sentences.

    1. Bob Brass looked <u>miserable</u>; in other words, he appeared to be tired, tense, and unhappy.

    2. If you can't find this spy, I'll soon be <u>bankrupt</u>; that is, I'll be so poor that I'll have to go out of business.

G.   Read Part 1 of the story again and check your answers.

Part 2: Fiction Reading (continued)

A. Picture clues. What do you think happens in Part 2 of the story? Look for clues in the pictures and then write T (true) or F (false) on the lines.

_____ 1. Sharon Holmes goes to work at Brass Designs, Inc.

_____ 2. The business manager of Brass Designs is a woman.

_____ 3. The employees are unhappy and unfriendly.

_____ 4. Sharon has an idea.

B. Read the second part of the story. Think about the mystery.

The Case of the Stolen Fashion Designs
(continued)

The next day Sharon Holmes went to work at Brass Designs, Inc. She hoped to find the spy quickly. Bob Brass introduced her to his employees and said that she was a new artist.

Sharon was glad that she took an art class each semester at the local college. She wasn't a very good artist, but at least she could pretend for a few days to be one; that is, she could act like an artist, and the other employees would believe her.

Every day for the next week, Sharon worked with the other employees. She took coffee breaks with them and had lunch with them. But she couldn't find any clues to lead her to the spy. Nothing unusual happened.

Everyone seemed very friendly. Bill Hanson—the business manager—was especially nice to her. He said "hi" several times a day and once brought Sharon some fresh fruit from his garden. Alice Lower—the secretary—said "Good morning" as Sharon walked in each day and helped her find the right materials—that is, pencils, pens, ink, and paper—that she needed for her drawings. And one of the artists, Eve Sumner, greeted Sharon every morning with a big smile and a handshake.

After two weeks at Bob Brass Designs, Sharon began to worry. She still didn't know the answer: *Who was the spy?* Also, she almost didn't *want* to find the spy because she liked everyone there.

At about noon one day, she turned to Eve, at the next desk.

"I'm going to lunch now, Eve," Sharon said. "Would you like to come with me?"

Eve shook her head. "Sorry. I can't. I'm having lunch with my sister. She lives in Thomasville—a small town in the Midwest—and she's visiting me for a few days. Maybe Friday, instead?"

"Sure," Sharon said.

"Oh, here she is now," Eve said.

Eve went over to her sister and greeted her with a hug. She kissed her on both cheeks. Then she introduced her to Bill Hanson, Alice Lower, and Sharon. They all talked for a few minutes before they went to lunch.

Sharon suddenly realized something. She ran to Bob Brass's office.

"Bob," she said, "are any of your employees from another country?"

"No," he answered. "Their application forms say they were all born in this country. Why do you ask?"

"Well," she said, "someone is lying. One person is from another country—Xenrovia. This person is the spy, and now I know who it is!"

C. Did you understand the story? Number these events in the correct order.

_____ Sharon asked Eve Sumner about lunch.

_____ Sharon worked with the friendly employees and began to worry because she couldn't find the spy.

_1_ Bob Brass introduced Sharon to his employees and said that she was a new artist.

_____ Sharon went to Bob Brass's office. She told him that she knew who the spy was.

_____ Eve Sumner's sister arrived and talked to people in the office.

D. Can you figure it out? Answer these questions about the second half of the story. You'll get more information later.

1. Why did Sharon go to work at Brass Designs, Inc.? Did the employees there know that she was a detective?
2. Who were three of the employees at Brass Designs, Inc.? In what ways were they friendly to Sharon?
3. Why couldn't Eve Sumner go to lunch one day with Sharon?
4. Why did Sharon run to Bob Brass's office?

E. Choose the correct definition of each underlined word. Use the pictures.

1. Eve greeted her with a <u>hug</u>.
   a. smile   c. handshake
   b. a wave of the hand   d. a "hold" with the arms
2. Then she kissed her on both <u>cheeks</u>.
   a. the mouth   c. the side of the face
   b. the forehead   d. the nose
3. Sharon suddenly <u>realized</u> something.
   a. did   b. understood   c. broke   d. finished

F. Find phrases after or between dashes in Part 2 of the story. Use the information to answer these questions.

1. Who was Bill Hanson?
2. Who was Alice Lower?
3. What is Thomasville?

G. Explain the underlined words in these sentences.

1. She wasn't a very good artist, but at least she could <u>pretend</u> for a few days to be one; that is, she could act like an artist.
2. The secretary helped her find the right <u>materials</u>—that is, pencils, pens, ink, and paper—that she needed for her drawings.

H. Read Part 2 of the story again and check your answers.

Part 3: Nonfiction Reading

Meeting and Greeting People

In the United States, there are many different kinds of greetings. The way two people greet each other depends on their age, their type of job, the amount of time between their meetings, the area of the country they live in, and so on.

People almost always shake hands the first time they meet in business situations. They use titles (Dr., Mr., Miss, Mrs., Ms.) at first but may ask that other people call them by their first names. They don't shake hands with people they see very often. For example, if they see someone in a business situation only once every ten months, they probably shake hands. If they work with that person every day, they don't shake hands. They just say "Hi," "Hello," or "Good morning."

At a casual (informal) party or social event, people often—but don't always—shake hands when they meet someone for the first time. In these casual situations, you don't normally shake hands with people you already know, even if you don't often see them.

If two women (or a man and woman) are friends or relatives who don't see each other often, they might hug; in addition, they might kiss each other on *one* cheek (but not on *both*). However, this custom is more common in some parts of the country than in others. For example, people in California greet each other with a hug more often than people in small Midwestern towns do. This kind of greeting depends on the individual people, too; that is, some people don't greet others with a hug because it makes them uncomfortable. They are not used to greeting that way.

People who met each other a short time ago don't usually hug or kiss. Two men hug each other only if they are close friends or relatives who don't see each other often. However, two men might hug when they are very, very happy about some good news.

A. Can you solve the mystery? Study the pictures (from Parts 1 and 2) and Part 2 of the story and answer these questions.

1. How did Sharon Holmes and Bob Brass greet each other when they met for the first time in Sharon's office?
2. How did Bill Hanson greet Sharon each day? How did Alice Lower greet her each day?
3. How did Eve Sumner greet Sharon each morning? How did Eve greet her sister?

B. Use the cultural information from this section to answer these questions.

1. Bob Brass thought that none of his employees was from another country, but Sharon knew that someone—the spy—was lying. Who was lying?
2. How did Sharon know that this person was the Xenrovian spy?

C. Discussing culture. Answer these questions. Try to use your new vocabulary words.

1. What are some ways that North Americans greet the people they see every day at work or school?
2. In your country, how do people greet each other at work or school every day? What titles or names do they use?
3. In your country, do people shake hands? If so, in what situations?
4. What is your opinion of greetings in the United States? Are you comfortable with American greeting customs? Why or why not?

Part 4: Writing

Using Capitalization, Periods, and Quotation Marks

1. Capital letters have many uses. Here are some of them. Use a capital letter:

   a. at the beginning of a sentence

      There were dark circles under his eyes.

   b. with names (of people, companies, or places such as cities, countries, oceans, deserts, rivers, etc.)

      Sharon Holmes
      Brass Designs, Inc.
      Xenrovia

   c. with days of the week and months of the year

      Friday
      April

   d. with the pronoun *I*

      If you can't find this spy, I'll be bankrupt.

2. Use a period at the end of every sentence that is a statement or a command.

   She hoped to find the thief quickly.
   Tell me about this thief.

3. Use quotation marks around the exact words that a person says. If you also give the speaker, add a *comma*.

   "I'm a fashion designer."
   "I'm a fashion designer," he said.

A. Here is the report that Sharon put in her file after she finished the job for Bob Brass. Correct the mistakes. That is, add capital letters, periods, and quotation marks.

REPORT: *The Case of the Stolen Fashion Designs*

on the morning of july 23, a fashion designer named bob brass came to the office he looked worried he had a serious problem somebody in his company was a spy from a clothing company in the country of xenrovia

this company is selling my designs all over the world, and i'm losing money fast, he said

i went to work at bob brass designs, inc. as an artist nobody knew my true job

everyone seemed friendly and polite -- especially bill hanson, alice lower, and eve sumner

after two weeks i finally found the spy, eve sumner i realized that she was really from xenrovia, not the united states

there were two clues that helped me first, she shook hands with me every morning xenrovians do this, but americans don't also, she kissed her sister on both cheeks most americans don't do this

of course, i told bob brass immediately, and he called the police

B. On the lines below, write sentences about *greetings* in your country. Begin each sentence with a capital letter and end it with a period.

Example: *Most women in my country don't shake hands.*

In my country, people bow each morning.

1. _____

2. _____

3. _____

4. _____

5. _____

6. _____

C. Choose one of the pictures from page 2 or 6. On the lines below, describe it in sentences; that is, tell what is happening. Be sure to use capital letters and periods correctly.

Example: *Two women are greeting each other.*

1. _____

2. _____

3. _____

4. _____

5. _____

6. _____

D. Choose another picture. What do you think the people said? Write quotations. Use quotation marks (and commas) correctly.

Example: *"Hi. I hope you're ready," she said.*

1. _____

2. _____

3. _____

2 Eye Contact and Handshakes

READING SKILLS:
Finding the meaning of a word in a following sentence

WRITING SKILLS:
Using *and*, *but*, and *so*

Part 1: Fiction Reading

A. Picture clues. What do you think happens in Part 1 of the story? Before you read the story, look for clues in the pictures on this page. Then write T (true) or F (false) on the lines.

_____ 1. The detectives' office is neat and well organized.

_____ 2. The detectives are happy.

_____ 3. Elliot Holmes is calling the Right Person, Inc. employment agency.

_____ 4. He wants to find a secretary.

_____ 5. He needs a secretary who can type.

_____ 6. It's not necessary for the secretary to do other things.

B. Read the story. Try to guess the meaning of the new words. Don't use a dictionary.

Who's Hired?

Elliot and Sharon Holmes sat sadly in their office and looked around at the mess. There were papers and books everywhere, the wastepaper baskets were full, and there was a pile of dirty coffee cups next to the coffee machine.

Their problem was lack of time; that is, they were working on so many cases that they never had any time to clean up the office. Also, they never had enough time to put papers away or type reports.

At the same moment, Elliot and Sharon both realized the answer to their problem.

"We need a secretary," Elliot said.

Sharon nodded. "Yes, you're right. We need someone to do the filing, answer phones, type reports, and greet people. If we have a secretary, you and I will have more time to solve mysteries."

Elliot picked up the phone and called Right Person, Inc. (the best employment agency in the city). He said, "We need a good secretary as soon as possible."

"Of course," said Wilbur Brown, the person at the agency, as he picked up a pencil to take notes. "Do you prefer a male or a female secretary?"

Elliot shrugged his shoulders. "I don't know," he said. "I don't think it's important to us. A man would be fine, or a woman would be fine. But we need a secretary with two essential, very important, qualities: politeness and honesty. Our secretary will have to be very polite to our clients (the people who pay for our help). Also, he or she must be very honest. We want a person who always tells the truth."

"Fine. I understand," said Wilbur Brown. "We'll send over several people tomorrow morning, and you can interview them. I'm sure you'll be happy with the person you hire for the job."

. . . To be continued

C.   Did you understand the story? Answer these questions about it.

1. Why was the detectives' office a mess?
2. How did Elliot try to find a secretary?
3. What were two qualities in a secretary that Elliot thought were essential?
4. What was not important about the secretary?
5. How will Right Person, Inc. help the detectives?
6. In your opinion, how will Sharon and Elliot choose a secretary?

READING CLUE

Sometimes the phrase between commas or in parentheses gives more information about the word before the commas or parentheses.

Example: "Of course," said Wilbur Brown, the person at the
                       agency, as he took notes.

The information between commas tells us that Wilbur Brown is the person at the agency.

Often the phrase between commas or in parentheses is a *definition*.

D.   Find phrases between commas or in parentheses in the story. Use the information to answer these questions.

1. What is Right Person, Inc.?
2. What does *essential* mean?
3. Who are clients?

READING CLUE

Sometimes you can find the meaning of a word in the next sentence.

Examples: a. Sharon *nodded*. "Yes, you're right."
                        b. "Yes." Elliot *nodded* his head. "I agree."

From these two examples, you can see that people *nod* their heads when they mean "yes" or "I agree." *Nod* = a movement of the head that means "yes."

E.   Explain the underlined words in the following sentences.

1. Elliot <u>shrugged</u> his shoulders. "I don't know," he said.

    shrug = _____

2. They looked around at the <u>mess</u>. There were papers and books everywhere, the wastepaper baskets were full, and there was a pile of dirty cups next to the coffee machine.

    mess = _____

3. He or she must be very <u>honest</u>. We want a person who always tells the truth.

    honest = _____

F.   Read Part 1 of the story again and check your answers.

Part 2: Fiction Reading (continued)

A. Picture clues. What do you think happens in Part 2 of the story? Look for clues in the pictures and then write T (true) or F (false) on the lines.

_____ 1. Elliot is interviewing people.

_____ 2. Three people are trying to get the job as secretary.

_____ 3. One person is a young woman.

_____ 4. The young woman looks directly at Sharon as she speaks.

_____ 5. The middle-aged woman is very pretty.

_____ 6. The young man is shaking hands with Sharon.

B. Read the second part of the story. Think about the mystery.

Who's Hired? (continued)

The next morning Sharon talked with each of the three people the employment agency sent. Elliot sat nearby, listened carefully, and took notes.

The first person whom Sharon interviewed, Molly Pearson, was an attractive young woman. She was not only pretty, but she had a nice smile, too.

"Could you please tell me something about your experience as a secretary?" Sharon asked.

"Of course," Molly said politely. She looked down as she spoke. "I went to business college for two years. That's where I learned to type and do filing. Then I worked for Max Jones (the fashion designer) for two years. After that I worked for a cardiologist (a doctor who helps people with heart problems) for a year."

"Do you enjoy secretarial work?" Sharon asked.

Molly looked off to the side. "Oh, yes."

The next person was Doris Kapinsky, a middle-aged woman. She was quite homely. Although she wasn't pretty, her eyes were friendly. When Doris introduced herself, Sharon noticed that her handshake was very firm.

Sharon asked her about her experience as a secretary.

"Well," Doris said, "I studied office skills in high school. There I learned typing, filing, and office organization. After I graduated, I worked as a girl Friday, a female assistant, in an office for two years. Then I stayed home and was a housewife and mother for almost twenty years, but now I hope to go back to work in an office. I like secretarial work very much." She looked Sharon directly in the eyes as she spoke.

The third person was Ron Clark, an attractive young man. He introduced himself and shook hands with Sharon very gently.

Ron had four years of office experience—one in a travel agency, two for the telephone company, and one in a department store. He was working at the department store when it went out of business, so he needed a new job.

When the three people left, Sharon and Elliot looked at each other.

"They all seem to be qualified," Sharon said.

"Yes." Elliot nodded his head. "I agree. They all have the necessary skills. But I suspect that two of them might not be very polite or honest."

Sharon nodded. "I think the same thing. This may be an easy decision."

C. Did you understand the story? Match the following people to the facts about them. Write numbers on the lines. (Each line will have several numbers.)

_____ Molly Pearson

1,7 _____ Doris Kapinsky

_____ Ron Clark

_____ Sharon and Elliot

1. was middle aged
2. was an attractive young man
3. had a firm handshake
4. went to business college for two years
5. had four years of office experience
6. listened to people who talked about their work experience
7. was a housewife/mother for twenty years
8. looked down as she spoke
9. worked as a girl Friday for two years
10. shook hands gently
11. thought that only one person was both polite and honest

D. Can you figure it out? Answer these questions about the second half of the story. You'll get more information later.

1. Who interviewed the three people?
2. Where did Molly look as she was speaking with Sharon?
3. How did Doris shake hands? Where did she look as she was speaking?
4. How did Ron shake hands?

E. Find words or phrases between commas or in parentheses in Part 2 of the story. Use them to help you answer these questions.

1. Who is Max Jones?
2. What is a cardiologist?
3. What is a girl Friday?

F. Use information in the second sentence to help you explain the underlined word in the first sentence.

1. Molly Pearson was an <u>attractive</u> young woman. She was not only
pretty, but she had a nice smile, too.

    attractive = _____

    Note: Do we use <u>attractive</u> only for women? See page 20, toward the
    bottom of the page.

2. She was quite <u>homely</u>. Although she wasn't pretty, her eyes were
friendly.

    homely = _____

3. I studied <u>office skills</u> in high school. There I learned typing, filing,
and office organization.

    office skills = _____

4. "I <u>suspect</u> that two of them might not be very polite or honest."
"I <u>think</u> the same thing," Sharon said.

    suspect = _____

G. Read Part 2 of the story again and check your answers.

Part 3: Nonfiction Reading
Making Eye Contact and
Shaking Hands

In the United States and Canada it's very important to look a person directly in the eyes when you're having a conversation with him or her. If you look down or to the side *when the other person is talking,* that person will think that you're not interested in what he or she is saying. This, of course, is not polite. If you look down or to the side *when you are talking,* you might appear to be hiding something; that is, it might seem that you aren't honest. However, people who are speaking will sometimes look away for a few seconds *when they are thinking* or *trying to find the right word.* But they always turn immediately back to look the listener directly in the eyes. These social "rules" are the same for two men, two women, a man and a woman, or an adult and a child.

 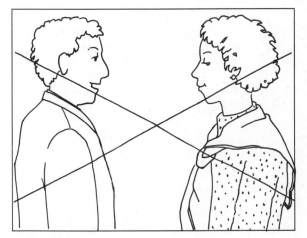

It's also important in the United States to have a handshake that is *firm* (strong). This is especially important in the business world. A handshake shouldn't be so strong that it hurts the other person, but it should be firm. Many Americans believe that a *weak* (gentle, soft) handshake means that the person also has a weak character and is not honest. This is true for two men, two women, or a man and a woman.

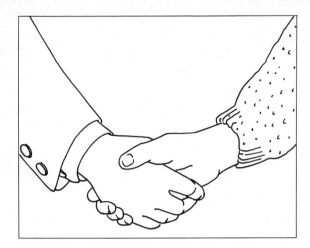 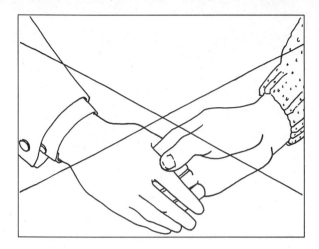

A. Can you solve the mystery? Study the pictures and the story (Part 2) and answer these questions.

1. How was Molly Pearson's eye contact?
2. How was Doris Kapinsky's eye contact? How was her handshake?
3. How was Ron Clark's handshake?

B. Use the cultural information from this section to answer these questions.

1. Which person did Sharon and Elliot choose as their new secretary?
2. Why did they choose this person?
3. Why did they suspect that the others weren't honest or polite?

C. Discussing culture. Answer these questions. Try to use your new vocabulary words.

1. What is *polite* eye contact in your country? Is it similar to eye contact in the United States?
2. In your country, what does it mean if the *listener* looks away during a conversation? What does it mean if the *speaker* looks away?
3. In your country, is the custom of eye contact the same for men, women, and children? If not, what are the differences?
4. Do people shake hands in your country? If so, are handshakes similar to (or different from) handshakes in the United States?
5. In your country, do men and women shake hands in the same way or differently?
6. Do you feel comfortable with the American customs of eye contact and handshakes? Why or why not?

Part 4: Writing

Using *and, but,* and *so*

You can join two complete sentences with a comma and a conjunction, such as *and, but,* or *so.*

and introduces more information; it adds one idea to another
but introduces information that might be surprising or unexpected
so = "that's why"

Examples: We'll send over some people tomorrow, *and* you can
interview them.
I was a housewife for twenty years, *but* now I hope to
go back to work in an office.
He was working in a department store when it went
out of business, *so* he needed to find a new job.

If there isn't a complete sentence after *and* or *but,* don't use a comma.

Example: They sat sadly in their office *and* looked around at the
mess.

In a series of three or more nouns, adjectives, or verbs, use commas between each part.

Examples: Elliot sat, listened carefully, *and* took notes.
I learned typing, filing, *and* office organization.

A. Combine the following sentences. Use *and* or *but.* Don't use a comma
or repeat the subject.

1. They had a lot of office work.
   They needed a secretary.

   _____

   _____

2. Elliot picked up the phone.
   Elliot called an employment agency.

   _____

   _____

3. We need a good secretary.
   We don't care if the person is male or female.

   _____

   _____

B. Combine the following sentences. In each case, choose the correct conjunction: *and, but,* or *so.* Be sure to use a comma.

1. They didn't have time to do the office work.
   They decided to hire a secretary.

   They didn't have time to do the office work, so they decided to hire a secretary.

2. Elliot didn't have time to do the typing.
   Sharon was too busy to do the filing.

   _____

   _____

3. Elliot liked to answer phones.
   He didn't have time for it.

   _____

   _____

4. Sharon interviewed three people.
   Elliot took careful notes.

   _____

   _____

5. Molly Pearson was pretty.
   She had a nice smile.

   _____

   _____

6. Doris Kapinsky wasn't pretty.
   She had nice eyes.

   _____

   _____

7. Ron Clark seemed to have the necessary skills.
   He didn't have a good handshake.

   _____

   _____

8. Doris Kapinsky seemed both honest and polite.
   They decided to hire her.

   _____

   _____

C. Combine the following sentences. Use commas between parts and use *and* before the last part.

1. There were papers everywhere.
   There were books everywhere.
   There were dirty coffee cups everywhere.

   _____

   _____

2. They needed someone to do the filing.
   They needed someone to answer phones.
   They needed someone to type reports.
   They needed someone to greet people.

   _____

   _____

3. Elliot nodded.
   Elliot smiled.
   Elliot stood up.

   _____

   _____

D. On the following lines, write sentences about the pictures on page 19. Use *and*, *but*, or *so* in each sentence.

1. *A young woman is sitting and looking at the floor.*

   _____

2. _____

   _____

3. _____

   _____

4. _____

   _____

5. _____

   _____

E. Write sentences about eye contact and handshakes in your country. In some sentences, compare the customs in your country with the customs in the United States.

1. *People in my country shake hands gently, but people in the United States shake hands firmly.*

2. _____
   _____

3. _____
   _____

4. _____
   _____

5. _____
   _____

3 Time

READING SKILLS:

Guessing meaning from context: using information after a semicolon; using information after *for example, for instance,* or *such as*

WRITING SKILLS:

Using *because* and *although*

Part 1: Fiction Reading

A. Picture clues. What do you think happens in Part 1 of the story? Before you read the story, look for clues in the pictures on this page. Then write T (true) or F (false) on the lines.

_____ 1. The detectives still need a secretary.

_____ 2. Doris Kapinsky is very busy right now.

_____ 3. Doris is daydreaming about detective work.

_____ 4. A rich woman is going to give a party.

_____ 5. The rich woman owns a famous necklace.

_____ 6. The name of the woman is Gigi Castle.

B. Read the story. Try to guess the meaning of the new words. Don't use a dictionary.

A Jet-Set Dinner Party

It was Doris Kapinsky's second day on the job as the new secretary for the Holmes Detective Agency. It was a quiet afternoon; there wasn't much work to do, and there weren't any clients to talk with. Doris was beginning to worry that her new job might be boring.

Then the phone rang. It was Penelope Ogden-Smith. Doris was very excited, but of course she tried not to show it as she connected Mrs. Ogden-Smith to Elliot's office.

After about fifteen minutes Elliot came out of his office with a piece of paper in his hand. He went to the coffee machine and poured himself some hot coffee.

Doris was curious; she very much wanted to know about Elliot's conversation with Mrs. Ogden-Smith. However, she knew it wasn't polite to ask.

Finally Elliot sat on the edge of Doris's desk, took a drink of coffee, and said, "Doris, we have a problem. The woman who just called needs two detectives to work for her on Saturday night. Unfortunately, my wife is solving a case in Chicago right now. Could you help me?"

Doris's eyes became wide and bright. "Do you mean that I can work as a detective?"

Elliot nodded. "Yes, but this will just be temporary; you'll do this kind of work for only one evening. After that, you'll have to go back to your regular office work."

"Sure," Doris smiled. "No problem."

"Good," Elliot said. "Now, here's the situation. Mrs. Ogden-Smith is having a big dinner party Saturday night. She wants us to keep an eye on everything; we're going to watch carefully and make sure that nobody steals anything."

"Okay," Doris said. "Where should we start? What should we do first?"

Elliot threw his paper cup into the wastepaper basket and stood up. "Well," he said, "first we need to investigate Mrs. Ogden-Smith and everyone on this guest list; for instance, I'll ask questions of their neighbors, and you can study newspaper articles in the library." He showed Doris the list in his hand.

"That's easy," said Doris. "Penelope Ogden-Smith is a widow; her husband died several years ago. She's very, very wealthy; for example, she owns dozens of buildings and three large companies, and people say she has over $20,000,000 in the bank. Most of her friends are in the international jet set; for instance, she knows a lot of movie stars, famous fashion designers, rich business people, and politicians from the governments of several countries. She owns a lot of expensive jewelry, such as the Stars of Siam, a necklace worth over $1,000,000."

Elliot shook his head. He was amazed. "How do you know all this?!"

Doris shrugged. "Easy," she said. "I always read Gigi Castle's articles in the "society" section of the newspaper. She writes about the jet set. In fact, she'll be at this party on Saturday. Here's her name on the guest list."

. . . To be continued

C. Did you understand the story? Answer these questions about it.

    1. Why was Doris Kapinsky bored?
    2. Why did Penelope Ogden-Smith call Elliot Holmes?
    3. Why did Doris get excited?
    4. What kind of person is Penelope Ogden-Smith?
    5. How did Doris know so much about her?
    6. How is Doris going to help Elliot on Saturday night? Why?

READING CLUE

Sometimes you can find the meaning of a word or phrase in the information after a semicolon (;).

Example: It was a *quiet* afternoon; there wasn't much work to do, and there weren't any clients to talk with.

We see that in this case, *quiet* means "not busy, not exciting."

D. Find information after semicolons in the first half of the story. Use it to help you give definitions of these words.

1. curious = _____

2. temporary = _____

3. keep an eye on = _____

4. widow = _____

READING CLUE

Sometimes you can guess the meaning of a new word or expression because there is an example of that word after the words *for example, for instance,* or *such as.*

Example: Most of her friends are in the international *jet set;* for instance, she knows a lot of movie stars, famous fashion designers, rich business people, and politicians from the governments of several countries.

The information after *for instance* tells us that the *jet set* is a group of rich, famous people from many countries.

E.   Find examples of the following words in the first half of the story and guess the meaning of each word.

1. investigate = _____

2. wealthy = _____

3. jewelry = _____

F.   Read Part 1 of the story again and check your answers.

Part 2: Fiction Reading (continued)

A. Picture clues. What do you think happens in Part 2 of the story? Look for clues in the pictures and then write T (true) or F (false) on the lines.

_____ 1. Penelope Ogden-Smith's dinner party is simple and informal.

_____ 2. There are expensive, special kinds of food on the table.

_____ 3. Everyone probably knows that Doris and Elliot are detectives.

_____ 4. Penelope Ogden-Smith has a problem.

_____ 5. Somebody steals money from the guests at this party.

B. Read the second part of the story. Think about the mystery.

A Jet-Set Dinner Party (continued)

Elliot and Doris had an appointment to meet Mrs. Ogden-Smith at her home at 6:00, one hour before the beginning of the dinner party. They arrived exactly at 6:00. Elliot was dressed as a bartender; he was ready to begin mixing drinks at the bar. Doris was in a black and white maid's outfit. Penelope Ogden-Smith met them at the door, introduced herself, and showed them around the house.

"This is the main room that you'll need to keep an eye on," she said. She opened a door off the living room. "This is where my guests will leave their coats and purses. I want you to make sure that these things are safe."

At 7:00 the guests began to arrive for the dinner party. Doris greeted them at the door, checked their invitations, and took their belongings, such as coats, hats, and purses.

It was an exciting evening for Doris because many well-known people were there. For example, at 7:05 one of her favorite actors arrived. At 7:10 a senator and his attractive wife arrived. After that a famous artist came with her husband, a cardiologist. At 7:15 two businessmen, a fashion designer, and several actresses walked in. As guests arrived, Elliot served them drinks from a temporary bar in the living room.

At 7:30 Janice Stern, a travel agent, came in. Penelope Ogden-Smith went quickly to her, and they hugged. Penelope kissed her on the cheek.

Janice apologized immediately; she said, "Oh, I'm so sorry that I'm late! I had a pile of work at the office, and then a client called just as I was leaving."

"Don't worry," Penelope smiled. "It's no problem. We'll serve dinner in a few minutes. Please sit down and have something to drink."

At 8:00 the last guest arrived. This guest, Alice Mack, introduced herself to Penelope and shook her hand.

"I'm Gigi Castle's assistant at the newspaper," Alice Mack said. "Unfortunately Gigi can't come tonight; I know this is bad news, but she had to interview a politician who arrived at the office a few minutes ago. She sent me instead."

"Fine," Penelope said with a smile. "Please come in. We're serving dinner now."

Two maids served the meal. There were wonderful gourmet dishes such as caviar and lobster, and all of the guests enjoyed themselves. After dinner Elliot and Doris served coffee in the living room. Several guests went into other rooms to look at the famous paintings on the walls. Penelope Ogden-Smith went upstairs for a minute. When she came back down, Doris could see that she looked very upset; her hands were shaking, and her eyes were open very wide.

"Mr. Holmes," she said to Elliot, "someone stole my necklace! The Stars of Siam is gone! Someone stole it! It was there just before the party! How could this happen? Who could possibly have it?"

Doris, who was listening, turned to Elliot. "Excuse me," she said, "but I think I know the answer to that. One of the guests at this party is lying about something; I suspect that Alice Mack is not really Gigi Castle's assistant in the 'society' section. I believe that she is the thief who stole the Stars of Siam."

C. Did you understand the story? Number these events in the correct order.

3

_____ Guests began to arrive.

_1_ Elliot and Doris met Penelope Ogden-Smith at her home.

_____ Everyone had dinner.

4 _____ Janice Stern arrived and apologized because she was thirty minutes late.

2 _____ Penelope Ogden-Smith showed Elliot and Doris the room for the guests' coats.

_____ Penelope said, "Someone stole my necklace!"

_____ Gigi Castle's assistant arrived one hour late.

D. Can you figure it out? Answer these questions about the second half of the story. You'll get more information later.

1. What did Penelope Ogden-Smith want Elliot and Doris to keep an eye on?
2. How were Elliot and Doris dressed? In your opinion, why did they wear such outfits?
3. Why was Penelope upset?

E. Use information after semicolons to help you give definitions of these words.

1. bartender = _____

2. apologized = _____

3. upset = _____

F. Find examples of the following words in the second half of the story and guess the meaning of each word.

1. belongings = _____

2. well-known = _____

3. gourmet dishes = _____

G. Read Part 2 of the story again and check your answers.

Part 3: Nonfiction Reading

Understanding United States/Canadian Concepts of Time

Time is very important in the United States and Canada. People who keep appointments are considered to be polite. However, there are different social rules for different situations.

In the business world, it's especially important to be on time—for a job interview, an appointment, or to work each day. For example, if an appointment is for 9:00, the person should arrive at exactly 9:00—or perhaps even a few minutes early.

In social situations, the rules are a little different. When two people agree to meet at a restaurant or theater, they should both try to arrive on time. In such a situation, it's not terrible to be five to ten minutes late, but the late person usually apologizes.

For a party, people should *never* arrive early; that is, guests should not arrive *before* the time that the party begins. For most parties, it's fine to arrive five to fifteen minutes late. For some parties (very casual ones), it's even acceptable to arrive thirty minutes late.

However, for a formal party—especially a *dinner* party—people try not to arrive more than fifteen minutes late. If they're later than that, they try to call first. Also, they apologize when they arrive late. It's impolite to be more than thirty minutes late for a formal dinner party because the food is ready at a certain time and everyone sits down to eat at that time.

A. Can you solve the mystery? Study the story and then answer these questions.

1. What time did Elliot and Doris arrive? Was this a business appointment or a social meeting for them? Were they early, on time, or late? Why?
2. What time did the party begin?
3. What happened at 7:05? 7:10? 7:15? Did any of the guests apologize at these times?
4. Who arrived at 7:30? Did she apologize? Was she polite?
5. Who arrived at 8:00? Did she apologize? Was she polite?

B. Use the cultural information from this section to answer these questions.

1. Doris said that Alice Mack wasn't really Gigi Castle's assistant on the newspaper. How did she know that Alice Mack was lying?
2. Doris believed that Alice Mack stole the necklace. Why did she think this?

C. Discussing culture. Answer these questions. Try to use your new vocabulary words.

1. In your country, is it important to be on time for a business appointment? Is it better to arrive early, on time, or late?
2. In your country, do people usually arrive early, on time, or late
   when they meet someone at a restaurant or theater?
3. What's a good time to arrive at a party in your country? Is it okay to
   be late? How late is *too* late? Do people call first if they're going to
   be late? Do people apologize if they're late?
4. Are you often late? Why or why not?
5. Do you feel comfortable or uncomfortable with the ideas about time
   in the United States?

Part 4: Writing

Using *because* and *although*

You can join two sentences with *because* or *although*. Use *because* to give a cause or reason. Put *because* before the part that gives the cause.

Examples: Because the detectives didn't have time to do office work, they hired a secretary.

The detectives hired a secretary because they didn't have time to do office work.

Use *although* in a sentence that has surprising or unexpected information. A sentence with *although* has two parts: one begins with *although* and the other has the information that is surprising or unexpected.

Examples: Although Elliot was a good typist himself, he hired a secretary.

Elliot hired a secretary although he was a good typist himself.

Notice in the examples above that there are two possible positions of *because* and *although* in a sentence: at the beginning or in the middle. When *because* or *although* is in the first part of the sentence, use a comma. Try to keep the noun in the first part of the sentence and the pronoun in the second part.

Examples: Because Doris and Elliot were working at the party, they arrived on time. (comma)

Doris and Elliot arrived on time because they were working at the party. (no comma)

In the example above, *Doris and Elliot* is a noun and *they* is a pronoun.

A. Combine the following sentences. In each one, choose *because* or *although*. Use pronouns if possible. Write each sentence in two ways.

1. There wasn't much work to do.
   Doris began to worry that her new job might be boring.

   a. *Because there wasn't much work to do, Doris began to worry that her new job might be boring.*

   b. *Doris began to worry that her new job might be boring because there wasn't much work to do.*

2. Penelope Ogden-Smith was very famous.
   Doris was excited when she called.

   a. _____

   _____

   b. _____

   _____

3. Doris was very curious.
   She didn't ask anything.

   a. _____

   _____

   b. _____

   _____

4. Elliot was amazed at Doris.
   Doris knew so much about the jet set.

   a. _____

   _____

   b. _____

   _____

5. Elliot didn't want anyone to know that he was a detective.
   Elliot dressed as a bartender.

   a. _____

   _____

   b. _____

   _____

6. Doris was excited.
   A lot of famous people were at the party.

   a. _____

   _____

   b. _____

   _____

7. Janice apologized.
   Janice was late.

   a. _____

   _____

   b. _____

   _____

8. Gigi Castle couldn't come to the party.
   Gigi Castle didn't call to apologize.

   a. _____

   _____

   b. _____

   _____

9. The detectives kept an eye on everything.
   Someone stole the expensive necklace, the Stars of Siam.

   a. _____

   _____

   b. _____

   _____

10. Penelope Ogden-Smith was upset.
    Her necklace was gone.

    a. _____

    _____

    b. _____

    _____

B. On the lines below, write sentences about concepts of time in North America. Use *because* or *although* in each sentence.

1. _Although it's important to arrive on time for a business appointment, it's usually acceptable to be a little late for a party._

2. _____

_____

3. _____

_____

4. _____

_____

5. _____

_____

6. _____

_____

C. Write sentences about concepts of time in your culture. Use *because* or *although* in each.

1. _It's okay to be an hour late for a party in my country because our ideas about time are different from ideas in the United States._

2. _____

_____

3. _____

_____

4. _____

_____

5. _____

_____

6. _____

_____

4 At the Table

READING SKILLS:

Guessing meaning from context: using details around a word; using information after a colon

WRITING SKILLS:

Using *when, while, as, after, before,* and *if*

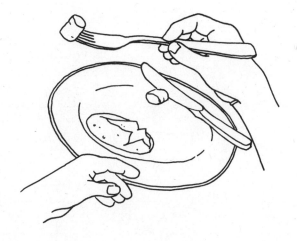

Part 1: Fiction Reading (continued)

A. Picture clues. What do you think happens in Part 1 of the story? Before you read the story, look for clues in the picture on this page. Then write T (true) or F (false) on the lines.

_____ 1. Sharon and Elliot are taking a vacation by ship.

_____ 2. They are on a ship with other passengers.

_____ 3. The captain of the ship is making small talk.

_____ 4. The captain is upset.

_____ 5. Someone is planning to blow up the ship.

B. Read the story. Try to guess the meaning of the new words. Don't use a dictionary.

The Hijacking of the Delphinus

Doris Kapinsky shook her head. "I don't understand," she said. "If you want to take a vacation on a ship, why don't you go on a cruise? Cruises are exciting; you can eat gourmet food, swim in the pool, go dancing, and maybe meet people in the jet set on your way to Hawaii, for example."

Sharon Holmes smiled. "Yes, but cruises are also crowded," she said. "There are hundreds of people on a cruise. Elliot and I need a quiet trip by ship, and that's why we're going on a freighter. We can rest, get a suntan, and catch up on reading: read everything we wanted to read all year but didn't have time for."

"But I thought that freighters carried freight: cars, televisions, food, and things like that," Doris said.

"They do. But each freighter usually carries ten to twelve passengers, too—not just freight—and Elliot and I want to be two of them."

Doris shrugged. "Well, okay. I'll call the travel agent if you want me to, but I'm afraid that you might have a very boring vacation."

"Good," Sharon laughed. "We *need* a boring week or two. *You* can keep an eye on the office."

Three weeks later Sharon and Elliot were relaxing by the small pool on the freighter Delphinus. They enjoyed the sun, the ocean air, and the people they were meeting. There were seven other passengers on the ship—four male and three female, all Americans. They had a variety of professions: one was a secretary, another a politician, another an artist; there were two businessmen, a mechanic, and a teacher. In the daytime some people swam while others slept or drew or read. But everyone came together at dinnertime.

It was in the late afternoon that the ship's captain came to talk with Sharon and Elliot. He looked upset. He spoke softly so that nobody else could hear.

"I need your help," he said. "You're both well-known detectives."

Sharon was curious. "How can we help?"

"It's a terrible situation," Captain Yan said. "One of the passengers is trying to hijack the ship."

"What?" Elliot was amazed.

"Yes," the captain said. "I found a note under my door a few hours ago. There's a bomb somewhere on the ship, and the hijacker is going to blow up the ship if we don't take him—or her—to Xenrovia."

. . . To be continued

C. Did you understand the story? Answer these questions about it.

    1. What did Doris think about cruises? What did she think about freighters?

    2. Why did Sharon and Elliot want to go on a freighter instead of a cruise ship?

    3. What country were the passengers from?

    4. Why did the captain come to talk with Sharon and Elliot?

    5. What did the hijacker want? What was he (or she) planning to do?

    6. What do you think will happen next?

READING CLUE

Often the details (small pieces of information) around a word can help you guess the meaning of that word. These details might come before the word, after it, or both.

Example: "If you want to take a vacation on a ship, why don't you go on a *cruise*? Cruises are exciting; you can eat gourmet food, swim in the pool, go dancing, and maybe meet people in the jet set on your way to Hawaii, for example."

The details tell us that a *cruise* is a trip for travelers who want to enjoy themselves on a ship.

D. Find details around the following words in the first part of the story. Then guess the meaning of each word. Write the meaning here.

    1. crowded = _____

    2. freighter = _____

    3. passengers = _____

    4. hijack = _____

READING CLUE

Sometimes there is a definition or a list of details or examples of a word after a colon (:).

Example: Freighters carry *freight*: cars, televisions, food, and things like that.

The details tell us that *freight* means things that people move by ship.

E.   Find information after colons that gives the meaning of the following words. Then write the meaning.

1. catch up = _____

2. professions = _____

F.   Read Part 1 of the story again and check your answers.

Part 2: Fiction Reading (continued)

A. Picture clues. What do you think happens in Part 2 of the story? Look for clues in the picture and then write T (true) or F (false) on the lines.

_____ 1. The captain is having dinner with the passengers.

_____ 2. Everyone is drinking the same thing.

_____ 3. Some people have their forks in the left hand, and others have them in the right.

_____ 4. Nobody is eating with his or her fingers.

_____ 5. Each person has a napkin on the table during the meal.

B. Read the second part of the story. Think about the mystery.

The Hijacking of the Delphinus (continued)

"Are you sure that the hijacker is a passenger?" Elliot asked.

"Yes. It isn't anyone on my crew; they've all worked on this ship for many years, and I've known them all for a long time. Unfortunately," the captain added, "I suspect that the hijacker is a Xenrovian. But it will be difficult to find him—or her—because all of the passengers speak perfect English."

Sharon nodded. "Yes, it *will* be hard. But we'll do our best."

"Good," Captain Yan said. "Oh, I forgot to mention one thing. Two of my crew members are looking for the bomb now. But the five of us are the only ones who know. Please don't tell anyone else."

An hour later Sharon, Elliot, and Captain Yan were sitting with the seven other passengers at the dinner table. They tried not to seem anxious, but it was difficult to smile, talk, and eat while they were nervous about the bomb and trying to solve the mystery. Which passenger was the hijacker?

Sharon and Elliot kept an eye on the seven passengers during the meal, and they noticed the different table manners—"styles" of eating.

For example, people chose a variety of beverages: wine, milk, coffee, and water. The two businessmen, the politician, and the teacher drank wine with dinner, but the secretary had milk, the artist had coffee, and the mechanic had water. Five of the people ate their soup quietly, but the teacher slurped his soup noisily to show that he enjoyed it, and the secretary didn't have any soup at all.

There was a choice of three main courses: chicken, beef, or a plate of vegetables. During this main course, the teacher and artist kept their knives in the right hand and their forks in the left hand as they ate. However, four others "changed hands"; that is, they cut their meat with the knife in the right hand and the fork in the left; then they put the knife down on the plate, changed the fork to the right hand, and took a bite. The secretary, who had chicken, picked up a chicken leg with her fingers. There seemed to be only one table custom that the passengers had in common. All of the people used napkins that they kept on their laps—not on the table.

After the meal everyone had coffee, and the artist had more coffee. Because there wasn't any cream on the table, the teacher snapped his fingers for the waiter.

"Could you please bring us some cream?" he said.

The waiter brought the cream and was pouring some more coffee for the artist when a crew member came quietly into the room. He gave a note to Captain Yan.

"Excuse me," the captain said to everyone. He quickly read the note to himself. Then he spoke very softly to Sharon, who was sitting next to him.

"We can relax a bit now," the captain said. "My crew members found the bomb a few minutes ago."

"Good," Sharon said. "And I believe that Elliot and I have found the hijacker. You were right. This person is Xenrovian."

C. Did you understand the story? What happened in Part 2? Write T (true), F (false), or I (impossible to know) on the lines.

_____ The captain thought that the hijacker was a crew member.

_____ The captain thought that the hijacker was from Xenrovia.

_____ Six of the passengers didn't know about the bomb.

_____ The passengers all had the same table manners.

_____ Everyone drank wine or water with dinner.

_____ It's very strange for an American to have coffee with dinner.

_____ The teacher thought that the waiter was impolite because he forgot to bring the cream.

_____ The bomb blew up.

D. Can you figure it out? Answer these questions about the second half of the story. You'll get more information later.

1. Why did the captain think that the hijacker wasn't a crew member?
2. At dinner, why was it difficult for Sharon and Elliot to smile, talk, and eat?
3. In your opinion, why did people have different table manners? What were some things that people did differently?
4. What information was in the note?

E. Find details around the following words or expressions in Part 2 of the story. Then guess the meaning of each word. Write the definitions here.

1. crew = _____

2. anxious = _____

3. slurped = _____

4. in common = _____

F. Find information after colons that gives the meaning of the following words or expressions. Then write the meaning.

1. beverages = _____

2. main course = _____

G. Read Part 2 of the story again and check your answers.

Part 3: Nonfiction Reading

Eating and Drinking

There is a range of possible table manners in the United States and Canada; that is, many very different actions are polite.

With either lunch or dinner, people choose from a variety of beverages. It's very common for people to drink just water, but they might also choose wine, beer, fruit juice, or milk. In formal restaurants people usually have coffee or tea after a meal, but in informal restaurants many people have coffee or tea with the meal.

North Americans *talk* during a meal with other people because they believe that eating is a social situation. However, they try not to talk when there is food in their mouths. Also, they try to eat quietly; that is, they try not to make any noises as they eat their food, drink something, or have soup.

People in the United States eat some foods with their hands: sandwiches, hamburgers, and so on. In addition, most people use their fingers—not a fork and knife—to pick up and eat a chicken leg or wing or meat on a bone (such as ribs). If it is a large piece of meat on a bone—such as a steak or half of a chicken—they use a fork and knife.

North Americans who are right-handed use a fork and knife in two very different ways:

1. They cut their meat or vegetables with the fork in the left hand and the knife in the right hand. Then they put down the knife, move the fork to the right hand, and take a bite. They do this for each bite.

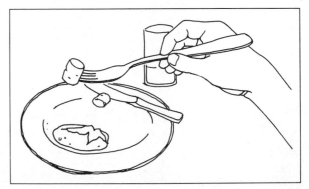

2. They keep the fork in the left hand and the knife in the right hand as they eat, and they take each bite of food from the fork in the left hand.

The first way is more "American," and the second is more "European." Some Americans use both styles of eating.

When people in the United States want to get the attention of a waiter or waitress, they try to "catch his or her eye." Sometimes they raise one hand a little or quietly say "Excuse me," but they *never* whistle (make a high sound through the teeth) or snap their fingers.

A. Can you solve the mystery? Study the story and then answer these questions.

1. What did each person drink with dinner? Was anyone's choice of beverage a strange one?
2. How did people eat their soup? Was anyone impolite?
3. How did people eat the main course? Was anyone impolite?
4. Who asked for cream? How did this person get the waiter's attention?

B. Use the cultural information from this section to answer these questions.

1. Who was the Xenrovian hijacker?
2. How did Sharon and Elliot know this?

C. Discussing culture. Answer these questions. Try to use your new vocabulary words.

1. In your culture, what do people usually drink with meals?
2. How do people in your country eat soup?
3. In your culture, do people use forks, knives, and spoons—or something else? How do they use these? Is it polite to eat with your hands?
4. Is it polite or impolite to talk at the table in your country?
5. How might you get a waiter's attention in your country?
6. What are very polite or impolite table manners in your country?
7. What are some other American table manners that you know about?

Part 4: Writing

Using *when, while, as, after, before,* and *if*

You can join two sentences with *when, while, as, after, before,* or *if.* You can use these words in the same way you use *because* and *although:* at the beginning of a sentence or in the middle. Use a comma if they occur at the beginning.

Examples: When Sharon and Elliot arrived on the Delphinus, they met the captain. (comma)
Sharon and Elliot met the captain when they arrived on the Delphinus. (no comma)

Sometimes the verb immediately following *when, while, as, after, before,* or *if* is in the present tense and the main verb is in the future tense. Both verbs have a future meaning.

Example: They'll take a cruise. + They'll be able to relax.
If they take a cruise, they'll be able to relax.

While and *as* both mean *when,* but people very often use them before a verb in the continuous tense.

Example: As (While) Sharon and Elliot were sitting by the pool, the captain came up to them.

Remember to try to keep the noun in the first part of the sentence and the pronoun in the second part.

A. Combine the following sentences. In each case, choose one of these words: *when, while, as, after, before,* or *if.* Use pronouns if possible.

1. The captain told them about the hijacker.
They were amazed.

    a. *When the captain told them about the hijacker, they were amazed.*

    b. *They were amazed when the captain told them about the hijacker.*

2. He began to eat.
He put his napkin on his lap.

    a. _____

    _____

b. _____

_____

3. She was eating.
   She kept her fork in her left hand and her knife in the right.

   a. _____

   _____

   b. _____

   _____

4. They will go to Xenrovia.
   The hijacker won't blow up the ship.

   a. _____

   _____

   b. _____

   _____

5. They'll find the hijacker.
   The captain will relax.

   a. _____

   _____

   b. _____

   _____

6. The passengers will eat.
   The detectives will watch them carefully.

   a. _____

   _____

   b. _____

   _____

7. He ate his soup.
   He made slurping noises.

   a. _____

   _____

   b. _____

   _____

8. They'll finish dinner.
They'll put their napkins on the table and get up to leave.

a. _____

_____

b. _____

_____

B. On the lines, write sentences about table manners in your culture. Use *when*, *while*, *as*, *after*, *before*, and *if*.

1. *When you finish with your chopsticks, you shouldn't put them in your rice bowl.*

2. _____

_____

3. _____

_____

4. _____

_____

5. _____

_____

6. _____

_____

7. _____

_____

8. _____

_____

9. _____

_____

10. _____

_____

5 Yes or No?

READING SKILLS:

Understanding a word from information that occurred before it

Understanding meaning when words are left out

WRITING SKILLS:

Using *however, therefore, in addition,* and *then*

Part 1: Fiction Reading

A. Picture clues. What do you think happens in Part 1 of the story? Before you read the story, look for clues in the pictures on this page. Then write T (true) or F (false) on the lines.

_____ 1. Elliot talks by phone with a man in Xenrovia who is president of a shoe factory.

_____ 2. The man in Xenrovia probably needs to find a manager.

_____ 3. Elliot goes to a restaurant with his wife.

_____ 4. Elliot and the woman in the restaurant discuss love.

_____ 5. Elliot and the woman talk about the plans for a new building.

_____ 6. The woman loves the building plans and is very excited.

B. Read the story. Try to guess the meaning of the new words. Don't use a dictionary.

The New Xenrovian Factory Manager

Late one afternoon Elliot Holmes got a long-distance phone call from a client in Xenrovia. His client owned the largest shoe factory in Xenrovia and was also a politician in the Xenrovian government. Elliot was happy to hear from him.

"Could you help me?" his client asked.

"I'll sure try," Elliot promised him.

"Well," the client said, "I'm planning to build a new factory in your city very soon. Most of the employees will be American, but the manager will be Xenrovian. I have three people in mind for the job. They're all qualified to manage a big factory, so I know that I won't go bankrupt if I hire any one of them. But it's important for me to give this job to someone who is honest and polite and—most importantly—who gets along well with Americans."

Elliot was curious. "But how can I help?" he asked.

"I'd like to send these three people to the United States for one last interview—with you—and I want *you* to choose the best person."

Elliot was a little surprised, but the job sounded interesting to him.

"Fine," he said. "I'll be glad to. How should we do this?"

"Here's my plan," the client said. "You're a detective, but I don't want them to realize that. I'd like you to meet each person separately—not all three together. Perhaps you can meet for lunch or dinner at a restaurant. You'll need something to talk about with them, so I'll send you a pile of possible designs that my architect has drawn for the factory. Discuss these with each person. Then decide which will be best for the job."

"Okay," Elliot said. "I'll do my best."

One week later Elliot sat in a restaurant with the first person his client was interested in. This person—a middle-aged woman—wore an attractive business suit and a few simple pieces of jewelry. Elliot noticed that she had very good table manners.

Elliot took out the building plans, and they discussed them. He picked up one of the plans and said, "I think this one is probably the best."

"Yes," the woman nodded, "I agree. It's very good."

"But we should make one change, of course," Elliot added. "We don't need to build this garden area with lunch tables for the employees. It isn't necessary."

The woman hesitated; she waited a few seconds before she spoke. Then she shrugged a bit and said, "Yes, you're right. It isn't."

. . . To be continued

C. Did you understand the story? Answer these questions about it.

1. What did Elliot's client plan to do? Why did he need Elliot's help?
2. What kind of person did the factory owner want his new manager to be?
3. In your opinion, why was it important for the new manager to get along well with Americans?
4. What did the woman say about Elliot's ideas on the new building?
5. Why did she hesitate and shrug a little before she spoke the second time?

READING CLUE

Sometimes a word refers to information in a sentence or paragraph before it.

Example: "Could you help me?" his client asked.
"I'll sure try," Elliot promised him.

Here, we see that *him* means "his client."

D. The underlined words in the following sentences refer to information before them. Write their meanings on the lines.

1. His client owned the largest shoe factory in Xenrovia and was also a politician in the Xenrovian government. Elliot was happy to hear from <u>him</u>. _____

2. I have three people in mind for the job. <u>They</u>'re all qualified to manage a big factory. _____

3. You're a detective, but I don't want them to realize <u>that</u>.

   _____

4. Elliot took out the building plans, and they discussed <u>them</u>.

   _____

> ### READING CLUE
>
> Sometimes a writer leaves out words because it's not necessary to repeat the information.
>
> **Example:** "Could you help me?" his client asked.
> "I'll sure try," Elliot promised him.
>
> Elliot's complete idea was: "I'll sure try to help you." But it wasn't necessary for him to say *to help you.*

E. In the following exercises, the writer has left out some words. Which ones? Write them on the lines.

1. " . . . I want you to choose the best person," his client said.

   "Fine," Elliot said. "I'll be glad to _____."

2. " . . . I'll send you a pile of possible designs that my architect has

   drawn for the factory. Discuss these _____

   with each person."

3. "Discuss these with each person. Then decide which

   _____ will be best for the job."

4. "We don't need to build this garden area. . . . It isn't necessary," he

   said.

   "Yes, you're right," she said. "It isn't _____."

Part 2: Fiction Reading (continued)

A. Picture clues. What do you think happens in Part 2 of the story? Look for clues in the pictures and then write T (true) or F (false) on the lines.

_____ 1. Elliot interviews the two other Xenrovians in his office.

_____ 2. Elliot goes to a Chinese restaurant.

_____ 3. Someone offers Elliot more food.

_____ 4. Elliot doesn't want any more food.

_____ 5. Elliot shows the architect's plans to another person.

_____ 6. This person agrees completely with Elliot.

B. Read the second part of the story. Think about the mystery.

The New Xenrovian Factory Manager (continued)

The next day Elliot and the second person had an appointment to meet at a Xenrovian restaurant near the office. Elliot noticed that this person—a man in his forties—had a firm handshake.

They talked as they ate the wonderful gourmet dishes.

"I'm glad to see that you enjoy Xenrovian food," the man said.

"Oh yes," Elliot said. "Very much."

The man offered Elliot a plate of fish and said, "Please have some more."

Elliot shook his head. "Oh, no, thank you."

"I'm amazed!" said the man. "You've eaten very little. Please take some more food."

Elliot smiled a little. "It's very good, but I've had enough," he said. "I need to keep an eye on my weight. I've recently noticed that I'm beginning to get fat."

"Oh, no," the man said. "I'm sure you don't need to worry about that. Here, have some more."

"No. Really," Elliot said more firmly.

The next evening Elliot met the third person. This man, too, shook hands firmly and had good table manners.

Over dinner they discussed the architect's plans for the new factory. Again Elliot picked up one of the building plans and said, "I think this one is probably the best. What do you think?"

The man looked over the plans and said, "It's a very good plan. I agree with you."

"But we'll have to change one thing," Elliot added. "We can't have this garden area with lunch tables for the employees."

The man looked surprised and curious. "I don't understand," he said.

"Well," Elliot said, "it's unnecessary and too expensive. Also, it might cause the workers to become lazy and spend too much time over lunch. Don't you think so?"

"To be honest," the man said, "I don't. I believe that people work harder when they feel comfortable and when the work place is attractive."

The next morning Elliot Holmes made a long-distance call to his Xenrovian client. "I've found the right person for the job," he said. "This person is polite and honest and will get along very well with Americans."

C. Did you understand the story? Number these events in order.

_____ Elliot called his client in Xenrovia.

__/__ Elliot shook hands with the second person from Xenrovia.

_____ Elliot shook hands with the third person.

_____ Elliot talked about the architect's plans.

_____ They ate Xenrovian food.

_____ The man didn't agree with Elliot.

_____ The man said, "Please have some more fish."

D. Can you figure it out? Answer these questions about the second half of the story. You'll get more information later.

1. What did the second person want Elliot to do? How did Elliot answer him? In your opinion, how did Elliot feel?
2. What did the third person say about Elliot's ideas about the garden?
3. Why did Elliot call his Xenrovian client?

E. Find information before each word in italics that tells you the meaning of the word. Write the meanings on the lines.

1. "Please take some more food."
   Elliot smiled a little. "*It*'s very good, but I've had enough."

   it = _____

2. "I've recently noticed that I'm beginning to get fat."
   "Oh, no," the man said. "I'm sure you don't need to worry about *that*."

   that = _____

3. Again Elliot picked up one of the building plans and said, "I think this *one* is probably the best."

   one = _____

4. "We can't have this garden area with lunch tables for the employees."
   The man looked surprised and curious. "I don't understand," he said.
   "Well," Elliot said, "*it*'s unnecessary and too expensive."

   it = _____

F. What unnecessary words did the writer leave out in the following exercises? Write them on the lines.

1. "I'm glad to see that you enjoy Xenrovian food," the man said.

   "Oh, yes," Elliot said. " _____ very much."

2. The man offered Elliot a plate of fish and said, "Please have some

   more _____ ."

3. "Please take some more food."

   Elliot smiled a little. "It's very good, but I've had enough

   _____ ."

4. "Don't you think so?"

G. Read Part 2 of the story again and check your answers.

Part 3: Nonfiction Reading

Saying *Yes* or *No*

In the United States, when people say "yes," they usually mean "yes." When people say "no," they usually mean "no."

When people agree with each other, they say so. But if they don't agree, they say that they don't. Often, to be polite, Americans will say a few words before they disagree or give bad news; this makes the disagreement or bad news seem "softer."

Examples: "To be honest, I don't agree with you."
"I hate to say this, but I don't think that's a good plan."
"I'm sorry to say this, but I don't agree."
"To tell the truth, I think you might be in trouble."

If people *say* that they agree when they really don't, other people might think that they're not honest.

However, sometimes Americans might choose to lie because they don't want to hurt someone else's feelings.

Examples: "Do you like my new sweater?"
"Yes, it's very nice."

"I baked this cake myself."
"It's very good."

If Americans don't understand something, they usually *say* that they don't understand. They don't pretend to understand when they really don't.

When Americans say, "No, thank you," they usually truly mean "No." Because of this, it isn't polite to ask Americans the same thing many times and hope that they'll change their answer to "yes." Sometimes a polite person will ask twice, but no more than that.

A. Can you solve the mystery? Study the pictures and the story. Answer these questions.

1. Who said he or she agreed with Elliot about the plan? Did he or she *really* agree?
2. Who disagreed with Elliot?
3. Who said, "I don't understand"?
4. Who didn't accept "no" as an answer?

B. Use the cultural information from this section to answer these questions.

1. What cultural mistakes did two of the people make?
2. Which person did Elliot choose for the job? Why?

C.   Discussing culture. Answer these questions. Try to use your new vocabulary words.

1. In your country, do people always mean "yes" when they say "yes"?
2. Do people in your country usually tell a person when they don't understand?
3. In your opinion, is it polite to tell people that you don't agree with them?
4. In your culture, do people offer food to a guest more than one time?
5. In your culture, do people usually accept "no" as an answer, or do they try to change the person's answer to "yes"?

Part 4: Writing

A. Combine the following sentences. In each case, choose one of these conjunctions: *however, therefore, in addition,* or *then.*

1. He was a successful businessman.
   He was a politician.

   He was a successful businessman; in addition, he was a politician.

2. This person is well-qualified to be a manager.
   I know that the factory will be a success.

   _____

   _____

3. He had three people in mind.
   He wasn't sure which one to choose.

   _____

   _____

4. He finished talking with his client.
   He called the restaurant to make a reservation.

   _____

   _____

5. Elliot enjoyed the food very much.
   He didn't want to eat any more.

   _____

   _____

6. The woman didn't agree with him.
   She said "I agree" because she thought that this was polite.

   _____

   _____

7. The man seemed to be very polite.
   He was quite honest.

   _____

   _____

8. They paid the bill.
   They got up and left the restaurant.

   _____

   _____

9. The employees felt comfortable in their jobs.
   They worked hard and tried to do well.

   _____

   _____

B.   On the lines below, write sentences about honesty and politeness in your culture. Use *however, therefore, in addition,* and *then.*

Example: *It's not polite to accept an offer of food the first time;*
therefore, a host needs to offer something four or five times.

1. _____

_____

2. _____

_____

3. _____

_____

4. _____

_____

5. _____

_____

6. _____

_____

7. _____

_____

6 Suggestions and Invitations

READING SKILLS:

Recognizing invitations and suggestions

Understanding the use of italics

WRITING SKILLS:

Avoiding and repairing fragments

Writing paragraphs (introduction)

Part 1: Fiction Reading

A. Picture clues. What do you think happens in Part 1 of the story? Before you read the story, look for clues in the pictures on this page. Then write T (true) or F (false) on the lines.

_____ 1. Sharon makes an appointment to help her client.

_____ 2. The person in the phone booth (Freddy Xenos) is probably upset.

_____ 3. In the detectives' office, Freddy is telling Elliot about a young man who is thin and wears glasses.

_____ 4. The young man looks happy.

_____ 5. The young man might be involved in a mystery.

B. Read the story. Try to guess the meaning of the new words. Don't use a dictionary.

The Missing Person

Freddy Xenos, a Xenrovian student, sounded very upset on the phone.

"Why don't you come by the office?" Elliot said. "You can tell me about your problem, and we can discuss it."

Freddy didn't hesitate before he said, "Yes, that's a good idea. May I come over *today*?"

"Just a second," Elliot said. "Let me check my appointment book."

A few seconds later he said, "Yes, today is good. Why don't we meet at 2:30? Is that okay with you, or do you have classes?"

"No, I don't have classes," Freddy said. "We started vacation last week; 2:30 is fine. I'll see you then."

Freddy arrived at the Holmes Detective Agency at 2:35. He apologized for his lateness.

In Elliot's office, Freddy began to explain his problem.

"I want you to find a missing person," he said. "I've been worried about this guy for *days*."

"All right," Elliot said. "Why don't you tell me something about him? How long has he been missing? Is this person a relative? And of course I'll need a photograph of him."

"Well, first of all, his name is Michael North, and he's been missing for about a week." Freddy thought for a second. "Yes, that's right. I haven't seen him for seven or eight days. He's not a relative. He's a friend; we take a computer class together two days a week. He doesn't have any family members here; they all live in Arizona. Hmmm, let's see. What else did you ask me?"

"For a photograph."

"Oh! I don't have one."

"Well, we'll have to do without it, I guess. Why don't you give me a description?"

"Yes, of course. He's tall, thin, wears glasses, and has brown hair. He's a little bald, too."

Elliot took notes as Freddy spoke. "Why are you worried about him?" he asked.

"Well, he's been very depressed for *months*—unhappy about school and his job. Although his family is very rich, he works part-time as a bartender while he goes to school and studies computers. I'm worried because he lives alone and is often lonely."

Freddy looked a little uncomfortable. "To be honest," he said, "I *was* afraid that maybe Michael killed himself because of his depression."

. . . To be continued

C. Did you understand the story? Answer these questions about it.

1. Why was Freddy able to meet with Elliot at 2:30 that day?
2. Why did Freddy apologize to Elliot?
3. Why was Freddy worried about his friend Michael North?
4. When was the last time that Freddy saw Michael?
5. What was Michael North depressed about?
6. What was Freddy afraid of?

READING CLUE

People often begin an invitation or a suggestion with the words *Why don't you . . . ?* or *Why don't we . . . ?* A sentence with these words can also be a polite command. The answer very seldom begins with *because.*

Example: "Why don't you come by the office?" Elliot said. (Elliot wanted Freddy to come by the office. It was an invitation or suggestion.)

D. Find sentences in Part 1 of the story that begin with *Why don't you . . . ?* or *Why don't we . . . ?* Write these sentences on the lines below; tell whether each is an invitation, a suggestion, or a polite command.

1. _____

2. _____

3. _____

READING CLUE

When people speak English, they often stress (emphasize) important words with their voices; that is, they say important words louder or more slowly (or both) than the other words in the sentence. Because writers can't "say" some words louder than others, they use *italics* (slanted letters) to emphasize a word.

Example: "May I come over *today*?" (Readers immediately see that the word *today* is important in this sentence. They can imagine that the speaker is stressing this word.)

Sometimes italics add meaning.

Example: I've been waiting for *hours*. (*Hours*, here, means *many* hours.)

E.   Find the words in italics in Part 1 of the story. Write them on the lines below and decide if they have an extra meaning or not.

1. _____

2. _____

3. _____

F.   Read Part 1 of the story again and check your answers.

Part 2: Fiction Reading (continued)

A. Picture clues. What do you think happens in Part 2 of the story? Look for clues in the pictures on this page and then write T (true) or F (false) on the lines.

_____ 1. Freddy seems pretty sure of what happened to Michael.

_____ 2. Freddy seems afraid that Michael might be dead.

_____ 3. Freddy seems afraid that maybe someone "stole" Michael.

_____ 4. Freddy is telling Elliot about a conversation with his friend Michael.

_____ 5. Freddy and Michael made an appointment to meet soon and wrote this in their appointment books.

B. Read the second part of the story. Think about the mystery.

The Missing Person (continued)

Elliot was curious. "Killed himself? You said that you *were* afraid of this—not that you *are* afraid of it."

"That's right," Freddy said. "I *thought* that he committed suicide, but now I think that he probably didn't. I went to check his apartment yesterday; the manager let me go in. Michael wasn't there, and everything was in order. Now I'm worried about something else."

"What's that?"

"I suspect that someone kidnapped him. I see it often on American TV. Criminals 'steal' a person from a wealthy family. Then they send a note that says, 'We'll give you back your son only if you give us $1,000,000.'"

"You mean ransom money," Elliot said.

"Yes. That's right. Ransom."

"Well," Elliot said, "*possibly* someone kidnapped him. Has anyone received a ransom note?"

"I don't know," Freddy said miserably. "His family in Arizona doesn't seem to be answering the phone. Where *is* he? I don't understand."

"Have you checked his work place?"

"Yes. I went to the restaurant. He quit his job a week ago."

"Hmmm," Elliot said. "Why don't you tell me about your last conversation with him?"

"It was a short one," Freddy said. "I saw him at school for a few minutes one day. I said, 'Why don't we get together for lunch some day next week?' And he said, 'Yes, that sounds like a good idea; I'll call you.' However, he never called, and I haven't seen him since then. When I studied at the International Language School last semester, I learned that *yes* means 'yes' to Americans, so I became worried when he didn't call."

Elliot smiled. "Why don't we go downstairs and have some tea? I think you need to relax."

Freddy shook his head. "How can I relax while my friend is missing?"

"Come on downstairs," Elliot said more firmly. "Over a good, hot cup of tea, I'll tell you where your friend is."

C. Did you understand the story? Number the events in order.

_____ Freddy went to check Michael North's apartment.

_____ Freddy had a short conversation with Michael at school.

_____ Elliot suggested some tea.

_____ Freddy thought his friend killed himself.

_____ Freddy suspected that someone kidnapped his friend.

_1_ Freddy learned about American culture at the International Language School.

D. Can you figure it out? Answer these questions about the second half of the story. You'll get more information later.

1. At first, Freddy was afraid that his friend killed himself. Why did he think that this was possible?
2. Why did Freddy change his mind about this?
3. Where did Freddy get his idea about kidnapping?
4. When Freddy and Michael spoke with each other at school, what did Freddy say? What was Michael's answer?
5. Why did Freddy become worried?

E. Find sentences that begin with *Why don't you . . . ?* or *Why don't we . . . ?* in Part 2 of the story. Write these sentences on the lines below. Then tell whether each is an invitation, a suggestion, or a polite command.

1. _____

_____

2. _____

_____

3. _____

_____

F. Find words in italics in Part 2 of the story. Write them on the lines below.

1. _____   4. _____

2. _____   5. _____

3. _____   6. _____

G. Read Part 2 of the story again and check your answers.

7

Part 3: Nonfiction Reading

Making General and Specific
Suggestions or Invitations

As we saw in Chapter 5, *yes* usually means "yes" and *no* usually means "no" in the United States.

However, sometimes *yes* doesn't really mean "yes." Sometimes it means "maybe" or "I'd like to but I can't." In these cases, people say *yes* because they want to be friendly and polite. One point here is very important, though. People use *yes* when they don't mean "yes" only in an answer to a *general* suggestion or invitation.

When the suggestion or invitation is *specific*, the person needs to be more direct and more honest.

If people say they'll call *soon, sometime soon, sometime next week, in a couple of weeks,* or at another general future time, it isn't certain that they'll actually call at that time—or perhaps at all. However, if they say they'll call *this evening, tomorrow, on Tuesday, next Saturday,* or at another specific time, they truly plan to call, and you can expect them to do so.

A. Can you solve the mystery? Look at these sentences from the story and answer the questions.

1. In the story, Elliot said to Freddy, "Why don't you come by the office?" Freddy replied, "Yes, that's a good idea. May I come over *today?*" When Freddy said *yes* to Elliot's suggestion, do you think he really meant *yes, no,* or *maybe?* Why do you think this?
2. Freddy said to Michael, "Why don't we get together for lunch some day next week?" Michael answered, "Yes, that sounds like a good idea. I'll call you." When Michael said *yes* to Freddy's suggestion, do you think he really meant *yes, no,* or *maybe?* Why do you think this?

B. Use the cultural information from this section to answer these questions.

1. Why didn't Freddy and Michael have classes on the day Freddy went to Elliot's office?
2. Elliot smiled and suggested some tea at the end of the story. He didn't seem very worried. Why not?
3. What probably happened to Freddy?

C. Discussing culture. Answer these questions. Try to use your new vocabulary words.

1. Do people in your culture sometimes say *yes* when they don't mean it because they want to be polite and friendly? If so, is the custom similar to the American custom or different from it?
2. How do people in your country politely say *no* to a suggestion or invitation?
3. Have you ever had a conversation with an American that was similar to Freddy's conversation with Michael? If so, did it seem unusual to you?

Part 4: Writing

AVOIDING AND REPAIRING FRAGMENTS

Many students have a problem with fragments when they write in English. A fragment is a part of a sentence. It looks like a complete sentence because it begins with a capital letter and ends with a period; however, it is not complete. It is fine to use fragments in conversation, but you should not use them in compositions or formal letters. There are several kinds of fragments, and a good writer soon learns to avoid each kind. Some possible kinds of fragments (and the corrections) are below.

Examples:

WRONG: Went to the office   [no subject]
CORRECT: He went to the office.

WRONG: He took off his hat. Sat down.   [no subject]
CORRECT: He took off his hat and sat down.

WRONG: The student walking across the campus.   [incomplete verb]
CORRECT: The student walked across the campus.
CORRECT: The student was walking across the campus when he saw his friend.

WRONG: In his office.   [phrase; no subject or verb]
CORRECT: They met in his office.
CORRECT: In his office, many clients told him their problems.

A very common kind of fragment is one with a subordinating conjunction such as *because, although, when, while, as, after,* or *before.* (See Chapters 3 and 4.)

Example:

WRONG: He called Elliot. Because he had a problem.
CORRECT: He called Elliot because he had a problem.
CORRECT: Because he had a problem, he called Elliot.

A.   Combine the following sentences and fragments so that you have one complete sentence in each case. There may be several possible answers.

1. Freddy picked up the phone. Called Elliot.   *Freddy picked up the phone and called Elliot.*

2. The detective took notes. While his client spoke. _____

3. I don't have classes. Started vacation last week. _____

4. Because my friend has been depressed. I'm worried about him. _____

5. He hasn't been happy. With his job. _____

6. The detective needed some information. And a photograph. _____

7. After I saw him at school. He seemed to disappear. _____

8. He thought carefully. Before he spoke. _____

9. Went to the restaurant. Checked his work place. _____

10. I'll tell you where your friend is. While we have tea. _____

B. Correct the following fragments. You'll need to add words in each case. If you have difficulty, check pages 79–80.

1. Usually means "yes." *The word yes usually means*

   "yes." _____

2. Sometimes means "maybe." _____

   _____

3. Because they want to be polite and friendly. _____

   _____

4. When a suggestion is specific. _____

   _____

5. Sounds like a good idea. _____

   _____

6. Trying to be polite. _____

   _____

7. Will give you a call. _____

   _____

8. Although he didn't really want to go. _____

   _____

WRITING PARAGRAPHS

A formal composition or letter contains several *paragraphs*. Each paragraph is a group of sentences about one main idea. This main idea is in the *topic sentence*.

Example:

Indent the first sentence 5 spaces.

The main idea is often in the first sentence (*topic sentence*).

Don't indent again until you begin a new paragraph.

> There are two kinds of invitations in the United States: specific and general. When you answer a specific invitation, you need to be honest and direct. If you can't accept the invitation, say so and give a reason. For example, you might say, "I'm sorry, but I'm busy that evening. Maybe we can get together another time." If the invitation is general, you might say, "Yes. That sounds like a good idea," even if you don't really think so.

Every sentence is about the main idea in the topic sentence. This is called supporting material.

C.   On a piece of notebook paper, write one paragraph about customs in your country. Follow the example and be sure to avoid fragments. Put your main idea in the first sentence. Choose *one* of the following topics:

TOPIC	SUGGESTED TOPIC SENTENCES
1. *yes* and *no* in my country	In my country, *yes* doesn't always mean "yes."
2. polite invitations and suggestions	Polite invitations are different in my country from invitations in the United States.
3. what to say when you can't accept an invitation	Sometimes it's hard to know how to politely say *no* to an invitation.
4. a problem I had one time with an invitation	One time I had a problem with an invitation.
5. a situation where it's best *not* to be honest and direct	I think sometimes it's best *not* to be direct.

7 Criticism

READING SKILLS:

Understanding requests or commands with infinitives

Understanding sarcasm

WRITING SKILLS:

Avoiding and repairing run-on sentences

Understanding paragraph form (review)

Part 1: Fiction Reading

A. Picture clues. What do you think happens in Part 1 of the story? Before you read the story, look for clues in the picture on this page. Then write T (true) or F (false) on the lines.

_____ 1. Sharon is meeting with a client in her office.

_____ 2. Sharon probably expected this person to come and visit.

_____ 3. Her client is worried about a hijacking.

_____ 4. Somebody probably broke into the woman's apartment.

_____ 5. Somebody stole the woman's TV.

_____ 6. Somebody broke the woman's stereo into many pieces.

B. Read the story. Try to guess the meaning of the new words. Don't use a dictionary.

Face the Music

Sharon Holmes was at home late on Saturday morning while her husband, Elliot, was playing tennis. She liked the chance to spend a few quiet hours alone. She was enjoying the newspaper over her morning coffee when there was a knock at the door.

"Oh, *great,*" she sighed unhappily.

She opened the door and saw a short, middle-aged woman. At first, Sharon didn't recognize her, but after a few seconds she realized that she was the Xenrovian woman from the apartment building next door.

"I'm sorry to bother you," the woman apologized. "You're Sharon Holmes, the detective, aren't you?"

"Yes," Sharon said.

The woman introduced herself as Maggie Consuelo Wong. She said that she needed Sharon's help. She spoke very loudly.

Sharon asked her to come in. She poured Maggie a cup of coffee, and they both sat down.

"About an hour ago," Maggie said, "I got home from the store. My living room window was broken, and my living room was a mess."

"Do you mean that someone robbed you?" Sharon asked.

"Pardon?" Maggie said. "You'll have to excuse me. I have a problem with one ear."

"Oh, I see." Sharon was careful to speak louder. "Did someone rob you?"

"No. Nobody stole anything—not my jewelry or the TV or anything. They just smashed my stereo into about a hundred pieces. When I realized that nobody was hiding in my apartment, I told myself to calm down. Then I just stood there and thought, 'Oh, *terrific.* Now I won't have any music until I buy a new stereo. That's just *swell.*'"

"How strange!" Sharon said.

"Yes," Maggie agreed.

Sharon thought for a moment. Then she said, "If nothing was stolen, the person must not be a thief. But why did he—or she—do it?"

Maggie shrugged. "Perhaps the person was simply angry with me."

"Do you have any enemies?" Sharon asked.

The woman shook her head and said that she didn't think so. She told Sharon that she was new in the city and didn't really know anyone; therefore, she *couldn't* know anyone who hated her.

"How long have you lived in that building?" Sharon asked.

"About a month."

Sharon asked Maggie to tell her about her neighbors.

"I know three neighbors: the manager, Mr. Bean; Mr. Ellison, a mechanic; and Mrs. Atwood, a young widow."

. . . To be continued

C. Did you understand the story? Answer these questions about it.

1. How did Sharon feel about being home alone?
2. What had someone done to Maggie Wong's stereo? How did the person get into her apartment?
3. What country was Maggie from? Why didn't she have friends in the city?
4. What three people did she know?
5. Why did Sharon need to speak loudly?
6. In your opinion, why might someone have wanted to break the stereo?

READING CLUE

Often people use the verbs *say, tell, ask,* and so on with an infinitive (*to* + verb) to make a request or command.

Example: Sharon told Maggie to sit down. (Sharon's words were a command: "Sit down.")

An infinitive after the word *asked* means that the command was polite. The speaker probably said "please."

Example: Maggie asked Sharon to help her. (Maggie's words were probably "Please help me.")

D. Find three sentences in Part 1 of the story that have an infinitive after *said, told,* or *asked.* Did any of these speakers say "please"?

_____

_____

_____

READING CLUE

Sometimes people use *sarcasm*. That is, they say something that sounds positive or kind, but they really mean just the opposite. In a sarcastic sentence, the speaker usually emphasizes one word. Most people don't think that sarcasm is very polite because it isn't direct.

Example: "This is just *wonderful*," she said when she saw the mess. (The emphasized word—*wonderful*—and the whole situation—the mess—tell us that her meaning was sarcastic. She was really thinking, "This is just terrible.")

E. Find examples of sarcasm in Part 1 of the story. What did each person really mean?

_____

_____

_____

F. Read Part 1 of the story again and check your answers.

Part 2: Fiction Reading (continued)

A. Picture clues. What do you think happens in Part 2 of the story? Look for clues in the picture and then write T (true) or F (false) on the lines.

_____ 1. Maggie Wong lives in an apartment building.

_____ 2. She has a neighbor on each side—one male and one female.

_____ 3. Both of her neighbors probably believe that Maggie's music is too loud.

_____ 4. Both of her neighbors ask her to turn down her music.

_____ 5. Maggie and her neighbors probably get along very well.

B. Read the second part of the story. Think about the mystery.

Face the Music (continued)

Sharon asked Maggie Wong to tell her more about these three neighbors. "Do you get along with them?" Sharon asked.

Maggie hesitated a moment. "Well, sort of."

Sharon was curious. "What do you mean?"

"I don't get along well with them, but we don't get along badly, either," Maggie explained. "Mr. Bean lives downstairs, in the manager's apartment, of course. It's on the other side of the building, so I almost never see him."

Sharon's ears were beginning to hurt because Maggie's voice was so loud.

"And the other neighbors?" Sharon asked.

"Well, unfortunately, I've had a few problems with Mr. Ellison. Although I kept an eye on his cat for a few days while he took a short cruise, he's been rude to me several times," Maggie said.

"How has he been impolite?"

"Once, he said to turn down my music. Another time, he knocked loudly on my living room wall; I don't know why."

Maggie suddenly snapped her fingers. "Of course! That's it! It's very clear!" she said. "Mr. Ellison obviously hates music. Maybe he broke into my apartment and smashed my stereo."

"It's very possible," Sharon said. "But tell me about Mrs. Atwood. Have you had any problems with her?"

"Oh, no," Maggie said. "She's very different from Mr. Ellison. She's a lovely person, and she enjoys music."

"How do you know this?" Sharon asked.

"She's often told me so," Maggie answered. "She has often said, 'Your music is just *terrific* at 5:00 A.M. on a Saturday morning.' And only two days ago she said, 'I really *needed* that music coming through my wall at midnight last night.' You see, the poor woman is depressed a lot, so music probably helps to cheer her up."

"I see," Sharon said. "I have one more question. Do you think that you can trust these people?"

Maggie put one hand to her ear and asked Sharon to repeat her question.

Sharon spoke louder. "You've said that you don't often see Mr. Bean. You explained that Mr. Ellison is rude but Mrs. Atwood is polite. My question is this: Can you trust them? I mean, are they honest?"

"Oh, yes," said Maggie. "I'm sure that I can trust them all. Even Mr. Ellison is honest . . . rude, but honest. No, they've never lied to me. I think I like the directness of Americans."

Sharon smiled. "Now I can tell you who smashed your stereo."

Maggie Consuelo Wong brightened up. "Really? Wonderful! If you can solve this mystery for me, I'll invite you over for a big dinner. I'll prepare my most special Xenrovian recipes."

Sharon smiled.

"And you can listen to a concert on my new stereo!" Maggie added with enthusiasm.

"That's *exactly* what I need," Sharon thought miserably, but she didn't say anything.

C. Did you understand the story? Match the people to the facts about them. Write the numbers on the lines. Each line will have two numbers.

_____ Maggie Consuelo Wong

_____ Mr. Bean

_____ Mr. Ellison

_____ Mrs. Atwood

1. was the building manager
2. had a hearing problem
3. was a widow
4. lived on the other side of the building
5. knocked loudly on Maggie's wall
6. said that Maggie's music was terrific
7. liked directness
8. wanted Maggie to turn down her music

D. Can you figure it out? Answer these questions about the second half of the story. You'll get more information later.

1. Why did Sharon's ears hurt?
2. Maggie said, "Mr. Ellison has been rude to me several times." In her opinion, how was he rude?
3. Maggie said that Mrs. Atwood was very different from Mr. Ellison. In what way was she different?
4. What does Maggie like about Americans?

E. Find three commands in the second half of the story that have an infinitive after *said*, *told*, or *asked*. Did any of these speakers say "please"?

_____

_____

_____

F. Find three examples of sarcasm in the second half of the story. What did each person really mean?

_____

_____

_____

G. Read Part 2 of the story again and check your answers.

Part 3: Nonfiction Reading

Giving Criticism

Sometimes one person (let's call him "Person A") bothers another person ("Person B"); he makes Person B angry or uncomfortable in some way. What can Person B do?

There are several possible answers. First, Person B might do nothing at all. This is common when Person A bothers B only one time—or in small ways. In such a case, Person B doesn't think that the situation is bad enough for him to tell Person A.

However, if Person B wants to change the situation, he needs to say something about it to Person A. What can Person B say? In American culture, if B is an honest person, he'll be direct with Person A. He'll say what's on his mind; that is, he'll say his thoughts.

Sometimes it's difficult for B to do this because he doesn't want to hurt A or make A sad. In this situation, B *will still try to be direct.* However, he may also try to be polite; he might say a few words to make his directness seem "softer." (See Chapter 5, page 66.)

A few people don't like to be so direct. Instead, they might be sarcastic and say the *opposite* of their true thoughts; they hope that other people will still understand them. This, however, causes problems. First, people might not understand that they are really angry. Second, people might *understand* them but also think that they aren't polite. Most Americans believe that they can't completely trust someone who isn't direct.

A. Can you solve the mystery? Study the pictures and the story. Then answer these questions.

1. Mr. Ellison told Maggie to turn down her music. Do you think Maggie really played her stereo too loudly? Why do you think this?
2. Maggie thought that she could trust both of her neighbors. What do you think?

B. Use the cultural information from this section to answer these questions.

1. Who broke into Maggie's apartment and broke her stereo?
2. How did Sharon know this?

C.   Discussing culture. Answer these questions. Try to use your new vocabulary words.

1. What are some common disagreements that people might have with their neighbors?
2. In your country, how does one person usually tell another that he or she is angry?
3. In your country, is it more polite to be *direct* or *indirect*?
4. Do you feel more comfortable with people who are direct or indirect? If someone is upset with you, how do you prefer to hear about it?
5. What do you think is a good way to tell a neighbor to be more quiet?
6. Have you ever had any problems with neighbors? If so, how did you handle them?
7. In your opinion, is it possible to be both polite and honest when you tell someone that you're angry? If so, how? If not, why not?

Part 4: Writing

AVOIDING AND REPAIRING RUN-ON SENTENCES

A run-on sentence is an incorrect combination of two sentences; that is, two complete sentences are joined with no punctuation.
There are five main ways to repair a run-on sentence.

1. Use a *period* between sentences and begin the second sentence with a capital letter.
2. Use a *semicolon* between sentences.
3. Use a *comma* with a coordinating conjunction such as *and*, *but*, or *so*.
4. Use a word or expression such as *because*, *although*, *when*, *while*, *before*, *after*, or *as soon as*.
5. Use a *semicolon* with a word or expression such as *however*, *therefore*, *in addition*, or *then*.

Examples:

WRONG: She was relaxing at home her husband was playing tennis.
CORRECT: She was relaxing at home, *and* her husband was playing tennis.
CORRECT: She was relaxing at home *while* her husband was playing tennis.

WRONG: She was hoping for a quiet morning alone she agreed to help the anxious woman.
CORRECT: *Although* she was hoping for a quiet morning alone, she agreed to help the anxious woman.
CORRECT: She was hoping for a quiet morning alone; *however*, she agreed to help the anxious woman.

A. Repair each of the following run-on sentences in two ways. There may be several possible answers in each case.

1. WRONG: She poured some coffee they both sat down.

   a. *She poured some coffee, and they both sat down.*

   b. *She poured some coffee; then they both sat down.*

2. WRONG: The woman usually turned up the volume on her stereo she had a hearing problem.

   a. _____

   _____

   b. _____

   _____

3. WRONG: Sharon thought for a moment about the situation she agreed to help.

   a. _____

   _____

   b. _____

   _____

4. WRONG: I've often helped him he's been rude to me several times.

   a. _____

   _____

   b. _____

   _____

5. WRONG: He lives on the other side of the building I don't see him often.

   a. _____

   _____

   b. _____

   _____

6. WRONG: An honest, direct person in the United States will sometimes give criticism he usually tries to do it gently.

a. _____

_____

b. _____

_____

7. WRONG: He knew that this wouldn't be a problem again he didn't
complain about it.

a. _____

_____

b. _____

_____

8. WRONG: She told them what was on her mind she suggested a way
to solve the problem.

a. _____

_____

b. _____

_____

B. In Chapter 6, you learned about paragraph form. Now use correct paragraph form to write one paragraph on another piece of paper. (Be sure
to avoid run-on sentences.) Your first sentence will be your topic sentence. Choose one of the following topics. Then use one of the suggested topic sentences, or write your own.

TOPIC	SUGGESTED TOPIC SENTENCES
1. giving criticism	I've never felt very comfortable about giving criticism.
2. giving criticism politely	I think there are ways to give criticism and be polite at the same time.
3. a problem in not being direct	I had a problem with a friend because I didn't tell him (her) about something that bothered me.
4. expressing anger in my culture	In my culture, most people try not to express anger directly.
5. sarcasm	People in my country almost never use sarcasm.

8 Family Life

READING SKILLS:
Understanding infinitives that show purpose
Distinguishing fact from opinion

WRITING SKILLS:
Using adjective clauses (1)
Writing paragraphs: supporting material (reasons)

Part 1: Fiction Reading

A. Picture clues. What do you think happens in Part 1 of the story? Before you read the story, look for clues in the pictures on this page. Then write T (true) or F (false) on the lines.

_____ 1. Sharon and Elliot seem to be in the kitchen of an elderly lady.

_____ 2. They probably don't like the lady.

_____ 3. Elliot is on the phone with someone in the police department.

_____ 4. The man on the phone is probably Canadian.

_____ 5. They're talking about a kidnapping.

_____ 6. Someone might have killed an elderly man with a gun.

B. Read the story. Try to guess the meaning of the new words. Don't use a dictionary.

A Family Matter

The morning light came through the window and fell on the breakfast table. It turned the white coffee cups to golden and was so beautiful that it made Sharon Holmes feel suddenly sad.

"I think I'm going to miss this place a lot," she said.

"And the people," Elliot added.

"Oh, *especially* the people," Sharon said as she smiled at Elliot's Aunt Grace, who was sitting next to her.

Sharon and Elliot had come to Xenrovia three weeks earlier to visit several of Elliot's Xenrovian relatives. Their vacation, which seemed much too short, was almost over. Soon they would be back at work at their detective agency in the United States.

Suddenly the phone rang, and Aunt Grace got up to answer it.

"It's for you," she said as she handed the phone to Elliot. "I believe it's your friend from the police force, Captain Asti."

Elliot recognized his voice immediately.

"I'm sorry to bother you," the captain said, "but we have a difficult case here. Could you and Sharon come to the police station and discuss it with us? Perhaps you'd be interested in hearing about it. Also, it's possible that you can help us solve the case. It involves an American family here in Xenrovia. There might be something about American culture that you can help us with."

"What's the crime?" Elliot asked.

"Well, right now, the only thing we're certain of is that a man is dead. It seems that he died of a gunshot wound in the stomach. However, something is very strange; the wound didn't look very serious, but he died almost immediately. At first we thought that it was suicide, but now we're investigating the possibility of murder."

"Murder!" Elliot exclaimed. "Who killed him? And who is—er, *was* he?"

"He was a wealthy American businessman, Samuel Horne, who was living here with his family. We suspect that the murderer was someone in his family."

Elliot shook his head. "Terrible," he said, "terrible. But interesting! I'm positive that Sharon and I would enjoy helping. However, we're leaving for the States in two days. We'd like to spend the time visiting with relatives."

"Yes, yes, of course. I understand," said Captain Asti.

Elliot hesitated a moment before speaking again. "But perhaps if it takes just a short time . . . ." He looked at his wife and aunt to check with them.

"Go!" his aunt laughed. "I know how you enjoy a good mystery!"

"We'll be there in ten minutes," Elliot told the captain.

At the police station, Captain Asti thanked Sharon and Elliot for coming and poured them some coffee. Then he began to explain the case.

"Mrs. Horne, the victim's wife, was next door when it happened," he said. "She was visiting with a neighbor when they heard the gunshot. They ran next door to find out what happened, and Mrs. Horne found her husband on the living room floor. He was dead. The murder weapon was next to him."

"The murder weapon?" Sharon asked.

"This," Captain Asti said. He pointed to a very, very old gun on the desk. "It was his own gun."

"But this is an antique!" Sharon exclaimed. "It must be over a hundred years old."

"Uh-huh. Mr. Horne had a large collection of antique guns. Some people collect stamps; Samuel Horne collected guns." Captain Asti shrugged.

"Well, we're sure that Mrs. Horne didn't murder her husband since she was with the neighbor," Elliot said.

"Yes, she couldn't have done it," Sharon agreed. "But why do you think it was murder? Why not suicide?"

. . . To be continued

C. Did you understand the story? Answer these questions about it.

1. What were Sharon and Elliot doing in Xenrovia? How did they feel about being there?
2. Why did Captain Asti call Elliot?
3. How did Samuel Horne die? What was strange about this?
4. What did the police first think about the crime? What did they later think was possible?
5. Who did the police suspect of murder? Who *couldn't* have committed the murder?
6. What was the murder weapon?

READING CLUE

Some words are used with an *opinion* or *theory* (an idea that might be true or might be false). Examples of these words are:

think	believe
seem	appear
suspect	perhaps
probable/probably	possible/possibly
maybe	may/might/could

Example: I think I'm going to miss this place. (opinion)

Some words are used with *facts*. Examples of these words are:

know	prove
show	clear
sure	proof
fact	positive
certain	

Example: I know I'm going to miss these people. (fact)

D.   Which of the following sentences are facts? Which are opinions? Write F (fact) or O (opinion) on the lines.

_____ 1. I believe it's your friend from the police force, Captain Asti.

_____ 2. Perhaps you'd be interested in hearing about it.

_____ 3. Also, it's possible that you can help us solve the case.

_____ 4. The only thing that we're certain of is that a man is dead.

_____ 5. It seems that he died of a gunshot wound in the stomach.

_____ 6. At first, we thought that it was suicide, but now we're investigating the possibility of murder.

_____ 7. We suspect that the murderer was someone in his family.

_____ 8. I'm positive that Sharon and I would enjoy helping.

_____ 9. I know how you enjoy a good mystery.

READING CLUE

Sometimes an infinitive (*to + verb*) shows a reason or purpose.

Example: They had come to Xenrovia to visit several of Elliot's relatives. (= They had come to Xenrovia because they wanted to visit several of Elliot's relatives.)

E.   Find infinitives in the story to help you answer these questions.

1. Why did Aunt Grace get up? _____

_____

2. Why did Captain Asti want Sharon and Elliot to come to the police

station? _____

3. Why did Elliot look at his wife and aunt? _____

_____

4. Why did Mrs. Horne and her neighbor run next door? _____

_____

F.   Read Part 1 of the story again and check your answers.

Part 2: Fiction Reading (continued)

A. Picture clues. What do you think happens in Part 2 of the story? Look for clues in the pictures and then write T (true) or F (false) on the lines.

_____ 1. Sharon and Elliot go to see Captain Asti at the police station.

_____ 2. They're probably discussing the weather.

_____ 3. The gun on the desk probably killed Samuel Horne.

_____ 4. Captain Asti probably suspects three people of murder.

B. Read the second part of the story. Think about the mystery.

A Family Matter (continued)

Captain Asti began to explain what the police had found out.

"At first, as I said, we thought that Mr. Horne had committed suicide. But after investigating we found out that this was a very angry, unhappy family. Each son and the daughter had a motive—a strong reason—for murdering Samuel Horne. We'll soon know more; the doctors are examining the victim now to find out exactly how he died."

"Tell us more about the three children," Sharon said.

"Of course," Captain Asti said as he took out photographs of the murder scene and of each person in the family. "All three were in the house at the time, each in a different room. Any one of them could have done it."

"But *why*?"

"Several reasons. First, because their father was wealthy, each family member was going to inherit a lot of money when he died. But also, each of these people had an additional motive. It seems that each of these three hated his—or her—father for a different reason."

Captain Asti pointed to the photograph of an attractive woman in her late twenties.

"Julie, for example, was the oldest child," he continued. "She was adopted; that is, she was not their daughter by birth. Her real parents had died, so the Hornes took her as theirs when she was a child. She may have had a difficult time as a small child."

"But her motive?" Elliot asked.

"We suspect that she's angry because she's almost thirty and still single. Her father permitted her two younger brothers to marry before her."

"And the others?"

"The middle child, Peter, hated his father also. Although the family is wealthy, Mr. Horne made Peter go to work to make money when he was just a child—and later as a teenager. When Peter was only ten years old, he had to fold newspapers and deliver them to people's houses. When he was in college, he had to work part-time as a waiter in a cheap restaurant. He must have been very embarrassed and angry about this."

"And the youngest son?"

"Victor moved out of the house when he was only eighteen years old; we don't yet know why, but this fact makes us believe that he, too, didn't get along well with his father. Also, he refused to go into his father's business although the old man had wanted him to. Now, what do you think? Which child is the murderer?"

Sharon and Elliot looked at each other.

"Probably . . . none of them," Elliot said.

"What?!"

Sharon nodded. "I'm almost certain that this is not a murder case at all—and perhaps not a suicide, either."

There was a knock at the office door. Detective Nomos came in and handed a paper to Captain Asti, who read it quickly and then looked up.

"This is amazing!" he exclaimed. "You're absolutely right. The doctor's report proves that nobody murdered Mr. Horne. And he didn't commit suicide, either. He died of natural causes; he had a heart attack while he was cleaning his gun, and the gun probably went off by accident!" Captain Asti looked amazed to learn this information. "But how did you know?"

Elliot smiled. "Well, I'd like to explain, but would you mind discussing this at another time? We'd like to get back to spend as much time as possible with our relatives."

C. Did you understand the story? Match the following people with the statements about them. Write the numbers on the lines. (Each line will have several numbers.)

_____ Samuel Horne

_____ Julie

_____ Peter

_____ Victor

1. was adopted
2. moved out of the house when he was eighteen
3. was a wealthy man
4. wasn't married
5. delivered newspapers when he was a child
6. didn't want to go into business with his father
7. was dead
8. worked in a cheap restaurant when he was in college
9. was the oldest of the three children
10. had a heart attack

D. Can you figure it out? Answer these questions about the second half of the story. You'll get more information later.

1. Why did Captain Asti suspect that Samuel Horne was a victim of murder?
2. What one possible motive for murder did all three children have in common?

E. Find infinitives in the story to help you answer these questions.

    1. Why were doctors examining the victim? _____

    _____

    2. Why did Mr. Horne make Peter go to work? _____

    _____

    3. Why did Elliot and Sharon want to get back home? _____

    _____

F. Which of the following sentences are facts? Which are opinions? Write F (fact) or O (opinion) on the lines.

    ____ 1. At first we thought that Mr. Horne had committed suicide.

    ____ 2. We'll soon know more; the doctors are examining the victim now to find out exactly how he died.

    ____ 3. She may have had a difficult time as a small child.

    ____ 4. We suspect that she's angry.

    ____ 5. This makes us believe that he, too, didn't get along well with his father.

    ____ 6. The doctor's report proves that nobody murdered Mr. Horne.

G. Read Part 2 of the story again and check your answers.

Part 3: Nonfiction Reading

Understanding Family Life in the United States and Canada

Children in the United States and Canada, like children everywhere, first learn about the customs, values, and etiquette of their culture at home, from their parents and other family members. Learning these beliefs begins in the first year of life.

One important value that American families teach their children is independence. That is, children must learn to have their own opinions and to make their own decisions. One way that they learn this is to have their own rooms; in many families, each child has his or her own bedroom. Also, many American children have part-time jobs. These jobs (such as delivering newspapers, helping with gardening, or baby-sitting) help the children make a little money; but, more importantly, the jobs help teach the children to be responsible for their own actions and to choose between right and wrong. Later, when children finish high school, they often work in stores, offices, or restaurants (usually part-time) to help pay for their college education. It's important to understand that teaching independence to their children is an expression of the parents' love and care.

Parents might make suggestions about their child's future, but they usually expect each child to choose his or her own career or profession. Most children don't choose to "follow in the footsteps" of their parents; that is, they usually choose to do a different kind of work.

Most children seem to "leave the nest" when they are between the ages of eighteen and twenty-one. They find their own apartments and jobs and begin an independent life. Some stay at home longer, and some return home if they have trouble finding work, but this is a little unusual.

Parents do not find husbands or wives for their children. Children choose their own marriage partners and hope that their parents like their choices. Some Americans marry quite young (in their teens), and others marry in their twenties, thirties, or forties—or not at all. It isn't important in American culture for the oldest child to marry first.

There are many changes taking place in the American family. Many years ago a "traditional" family consisted of two parents and their children. The father worked outside the home, and the mother was a housewife. Nowadays more and more women also have jobs outside the home either because the family needs the money or because the women enjoy their careers—or for both reasons. In such a situation, preschool children usually go to day-care centers. Many couples decide not to have children; others choose to adopt a baby or young child; these decisions are not unusual. There are also more and more single-parent families due to divorce and to adults who have chosen not to marry but still want to have children.

Most elderly people who have retired from their jobs receive money each month from pension plans (from their work place) or Social Security. This isn't a lot of money, but it helps them continue to be independent. Although some elderly people feel very lonely and separated from their families, most choose to be as independent as possible. They enjoy their families, but they also enjoy living alone. They have their own friends and activities—such as art, exercise, and movies—at senior citizens' centers.

A. Can you solve the mystery? Study Part 2 of the story and answer these questions.

1. In Captain Asti's opinion, why was Julie angry with her father?
2. Why did he think that Peter hated his father?
3. What two things did Victor do that made Captain Asti believe he hated his father?

B. Use the cultural information from this section to answer these questions.

1. Is it probable that any of the children hated their father?
2. How did Sharon and Elliot figure out that there was no murder?

C. Discussing culture. Answer these questions. Try to use your new vocabulary words.

1. Is adoption common in your country? Why or why not?
2. Do parents in your country choose husbands and wives for their children? Does the oldest child usually marry first?
3. Do children and teenagers in your country have part-time jobs? If so, what kind?
4. Do children in your country move away from home when they finish high school or college?
5. What do you think about the importance of independence in American families? What value is especially important to families in your country?

Part 4: Writing

USING ADJECTIVE CLAUSES (1)

You can use an *adjective clause* to modify (describe) a noun. An adjective clause adds information to a sentence. If the information in the adjective clause is essential (necessary), there are no commas. Adjective clauses might begin with *who* (for people), *which* or *that* (for things), or *whose* (for possessives). These clauses come after the noun.

Examples: One important value that Americans teach their children is independence. (The adjective clause modifies the subject, *value*.)

They called the girl who sometimes baby-sat for them. (The adjective clause modifies the object, *girl*.)

An elderly person whose Social Security check is late might worry about it. (The adjective clause modifies the subject, *elderly person*.)

A. Find the adjective clause in these sentences. Underline it and draw an arrow (⌒) to the word that it modifies.

1. Children who have their own bedrooms have to learn how to keep them clean.

2. Many children have part-time jobs that teach them responsibility.

3. Parents whose jobs keep them away from home during the day find day-care centers for their young children.

4. It's unusual to find children who are still living at home when they are twenty-five or thirty.

5. Senior citizens' centers that offer a variety of activities can give elderly people the chance to make new friends.

6. Most people who get a divorce marry again.

7. Many couples who can't have their own children decide to adopt.

8. Many elderly people live on money that they have been putting into a pension fund for many years.

113

B. Combine the following sentences. Make the second one of each pair into an adjective clause and add it to the first. Follow the example.

1. The policeman needed some advice.
   The policeman called.

   The policeman who called needed some advice.

   _____

2. The light was beautiful.
   The light fell across the breakfast table.

   _____

   _____

3. They asked about the man.
   The man's murder was the subject of their investigation.

   _____

   _____

4. He picked up the gun.
   The gun had belonged to Mr. Horne.

   _____

   _____

5. The photographs were lying on the desk.
   The police had taken the photographs.

   _____

   _____

6. The woman was crying.
   The woman's husband had died.

   _____

   _____

7. The doctors wrote a careful report.
   The doctors had examined Mr. Horne.

   _____

   _____

8. He read the report.
   The detective had brought it in.

   _____

   _____

9. She asked about the boy.
   The boy delivered their newspaper each day.

   _____

   _____

10. The case wasn't really a murder at all.
    They were discussing the case.

    _____

    _____

WRITING PARAGRAPHS: SUPPORTING MATERIAL (REASONS)

As you learned in Chapters 6 and 7, a paragraph has several sentences (supporting sentences) about a _topic sentence_. There can be different kinds of supporting material; often, supporting sentences give _reasons_.

Example:

Topic Sentence	Many elderly people in the United States do not live with their children or grandchildren. One reason for this is a need for independence; elderly
Supporting Sentence (Reason 1)	Americans, like most other Americans, don't want to be dependent on other people and prefer to keep their own homes.
Supporting Sentence (Reason 2)	Another reason is that many elderly Americans choose to live in retirement communities. These communities are safe and quiet; they offer social activities and the friendship of other people of the same age.
Supporting Sentence (Reason 3)	However, some elderly people live in nursing homes (although they might prefer to live with their children) because they're sick. In a home where each person goes to work or school each day, it's very difficult to care for a sick parent or grandparent.

C. On another piece of paper, write one paragraph about family life in your country. Choose one of the following topics and write a topic sentence about it. (Your first sentence will be your topic sentence.) Then write supporting sentences that are *reasons*. Follow the example.

SUGGESTED TOPICS

family size
the choice of a career/profession
leaving home
a good age to marry
housework
children's education
choosing a husband/wife
divorce
the care of preschool children

9 Work

READING SKILLS:

Understanding the use of quotation marks

Understanding indirect speech

WRITING SKILLS:

Using adjective clauses (2)

Writing paragraphs: supporting material (examples)

Part 1: Fiction Reading

A. Picture clues. What do you think happens in Part 1 of the story? Before you read the story, look for clues in the pictures on this page. Then write T (true) or F (false) on the lines.

_____ 1. It seems that someone has stolen a painting and some jewelry from a museum.

_____ 2. The man at the desk probably likes art.

_____ 3. Time is not very important to this man.

_____ 4. Sharon is making an appointment with the man for 1:45.

B. Read the story. Try to guess the meaning of the new words. Don't use a dictionary.

Time for Crime

One May morning Sharon got an anxious phone call from the president of the Eversafe Insurance Company. He asked her to investigate a robbery at the city art museum.

"Yesterday morning someone stole a very valuable painting (*The Winds of March*) and a collection of antique jewelry from the museum," he said. He explained that his company would have to pay over a million dollars to the museum if no one found the stolen pieces.

Sharon promised that she would begin to look into the robbery immediately. As soon as she hung up the phone, she called Doris, the secretary, into her office. She told Doris to go to the library and find some information about the stolen jewelry and painting.

"What kind of information should I look for?" Doris asked.

Sharon shook her head and frowned slightly. "I really have no idea. I suppose I'd just like to figure out *why* the thief chose *those* specific pieces."

"Okay. I'll do whatever I can," Doris promised as she walked out the door.

When she had left, Sharon called Brandon O'Neill, the curator (manager) of the art museum. He sounded very upset.

"Oh, Ms. Holmes," he said, "I certainly hope you can find the stolen pieces very soon. We're all so worried! Until yesterday, no one had ever robbed this museum. The city art museum has been very successful while I've been here. We have a fine art collection and well-qualified people who work here. Also—I'm proud to say—this museum has actually been *making* money at a time when many museums are going bankrupt. Please find the thieves quickly."

"I'll try," she promised. "I'll need to come and examine the scene of the crime and talk with you and your employees. I'd like to do this as soon as possible—perhaps this afternoon at about 2:00?"

"Ms. Holmes," Brandon O'Neill said firmly, "I never use the word *about* when I make an appointment. I am on time, and I expect others to be on time. As you know, 'Time is money.' It's not possible to be a success in any business if you waste either time or money. Let's make our appointment for 1:45—exactly."

Sharon told him that 1:45 was fine, and she wrote it in her appointment book.

"Oh, one more thing," Sharon said. "Are there any suspects?"

"*Too* many," was the answer. "The thief might have been one of the museum guards or tour guides or a professional art thief such as Willie ('The Cat') Brown, who got out of prison last month. Or *anyone*."

Just a few seconds after she hung up, the phone rang, and a voice on the other end said, "Hi Sharon. This is Connie Willis. Do you remember me?"

Sharon was amazed. Constance ("Connie") and her family had lived next door to Sharon's family when the two girls were teenagers. They had gone to high school together. Although they hadn't seen each other for almost ten years, Sharon would have recognized her voice immediately even if Connie hadn't given her name. Sharon was very happy to hear from her.

"What a wonderful surprise!" she exclaimed. "I hope this is a social call and not a business one. You're not in 'hot water,' are you, or involved in some kind of crime and in need of a detective?"

. . . To be continued

C. Did you understand the story? Answer these questions about it.

1. Who hired Sharon? What did he want her to do?
2. What had someone stolen?
3. Who was Brandon O'Neill? What kind of businessman did he seem to be?
4. What were O'Neill's ideas about time?
5. Whom did O'Neill suspect might be the thief?
6. From whom did Sharon get a surprise phone call? How did she feel about this call?

"The museum opened at 10:00," O'Neill said, "and everything was in order at that time. But at 10:15, Charlie—the guard for this area—noticed the broken glass case. A few minutes later, Renée—one of the tour guides—saw that the painting had disappeared. The robbery must have happened between 10:00 and 10:15, while they were in other rooms."

"And these two people came immediately to your office to tell you?"

O'Neill answered that he had actually found out several minutes later, as he arrived at the museum. "I usually get here at 9:00, but yesterday I ran into an old friend just by chance on my way to work. Of course, I stopped to talk with him, and we had a cup of coffee. He was the one who told me about Willie Brown getting out of prison. Say, do you suppose that Willie Brown could have done it?"

The next morning, Sharon met her friend Connie Willis at her hotel. They hugged each other happily and then they went into the coffee shop, where they could sit and visit.

"Before anything else," Connie said, "you must tell me about your case. I'm so curious! How's it going?"

Sharon smiled. "You mean, 'How *did* it go?' It's all over. I found the thief, and the police made the arrest."

C. Did you understand the story? Write T (true), F (false), or I (impossible to know) on the lines.

_____ 1. Connie Willis called Sharon and told her that she was going to arrive later that day.

_____ 2. Connie was a little embarrassed to be giving Sharon such "short notice."

_____ 3. Connie was hoping to see Sharon during her time in the city.

_____ 4. Sharon changed her work schedule so that she could meet her old friend Connie.

_____ 5. The motive for stealing the painting *The Winds of March* was money.

_____ 6. Connie thinks Sharon is impolite for not meeting her at the airport.

D. Can you figure it out? Answer these questions about the second half of the story. You'll get more information later.

1. What was probably the motive for stealing the jewelry? Can you think of a possible motive for someone to steal the painting?
2. Where was the guard, Charlie, at the time of the robbery? Where was the tour guide, Renée, at the time?
3. Where was the curator, O'Neill, at the time of the robbery? What was he doing?

E. Tell the reason for each set of quotation marks in the following sentences. (See Reading Clue, p. 121, for help.)

1. "My only 'crime' these days is a short trip," Connie said.

   _____   _____

2. "I love a good 'who-done-it.'"

   _____   _____

3. Sharon smiled at her friend's question. "You mean, 'How *did* it go?'" she said.

   _____   _____

F. Identify each of the following indirect quotations. Write *command*, *statement*, or *question* on the lines.

_____ 1. She asked Connie when she was going to arrive.

_____ 2. She explained that she had an appointment with a client at 1:45 and would probably be working on the case until late in the evening.

_____ 3. She asked where Connie was going to stay.

_____ 4. She told Doris to keep an eye on the office.

_____ 5. O'Neill answered that he had actually found out several minutes later.

G. Read Part 2 of the story again and check your answers.

Part 3: Nonfiction Reading

Understanding United States and Canadian Attitudes Toward Work

Work is very important to most Americans and Canadians. A job not only provides them with a paycheck, but it also gives them a sense of identity. The first question that an American usually asks a person he has just met is, "What do you do?"

There are two possible historical reasons for this importance that Americans place on work. First, the Puritans (early English people in America) were very religious, and one strong belief of their religion was that work was both necessary and morally *good*. Second, both the United States and Canada are countries of immigrants. Most immigrants need to work especially hard when they first arrive in their new country to be able to survive and to make a good life for their children.

Even when Americans are not "on the job," they usually keep very busy. If you ask an American, "What did you do over the weekend?" he or she may answer, "Oh, nothing." However, this might not mean that he or she truly did nothing. This person may have done the shopping, worked in the yard, written some letters, washed the car, gone jogging, called a few friends, and seen a movie. But the answer, "nothing," means "nothing *special*, nothing *unusual*."

Most Americans feel they need to be busy in order to be happy. They don't like to "sit around and do nothing." Even their methods of relaxation sometimes involve a lot of activity. An American might "relax" by participating in a sport, for example.

Work is a high priority for most Americans and Canadians; that is, it is something that they believe needs to come first, before almost anything else. They might not enjoy it, but they still believe that "work comes before play," or "business before pleasure." American students usually have this attitude toward school, too. For example, if American high school or college students on their way to class run into (meet by accident) a friend, they'll usually greet the friend, say a few words, and then say, "Well, I've got to go. I have a class." This is not impolite at all. If friends want to visit, they'll arrange to meet at another time, *after* class.

An American doesn't expect a friend to make a change in his or her work schedule to get together for a visit—either planned or accidental. Friends plan times to see each other when neither one is working. It's impolite for people to expect a friend to be late for work or class—or to miss a day of work—in order to spend time together. This is, perhaps, especially true in the business world, where it is essential for people to show that they are responsible.

It's important to note that the priority of work doesn't mean that work is more important to Americans than friendship is. It simply means that in terms of time and schedules, work usually comes before other things.

A. Can you solve the mystery? Study Part 2 of the story and answer these questions.

1. Why was Connie Willis "sort of embarrassed"?
2. Why didn't Sharon meet her friend Connie at the airport?
3. In your opinion, did Brandon O'Neill appear to be a responsible businessperson?
4. Where did Brandon O'Neill say he had been at the time of the robbery? What was he doing?

B. Use the cultural information from this section to answer these questions.

1. Was it strange—or impolite—that Sharon didn't offer to pick her friend up at the airport? Why or why not?
2. What lie did Brandon O'Neill tell?
3. Who was the thief? How do you know?

C. Discussing culture. Answer these questions. Try to use your new vocabulary words.

1. What proverbs or expressions do you have about work in your language?
2. What kinds of things do you usually do in your free time? How do you relax?
3. Are American ideas about keeping "busy" different from ideas in your culture?
4. In your culture, what do you do if you run into a friend on your way to work or school?

Part 4: Writing

USING ADJECTIVE CLAUSES (2)

As you saw in Chapter 8, you can modify a noun with an adjective clause. If the adjective clause adds information that is not essential, there is a comma or commas. A nonessential adjective clause might begin with *who* (for people), *which* (for things), or *whose* (for possessives).

Examples: Connie called Sharon Holmes, <u>who had been her neighbor many years earlier.</u> (The adjective clause modifies the object, Sharon Holmes. There is one comma—at the beginning of the clause—because this clause is at the end of the sentence.)

The Winds of March, <u>which was a valuable nineteenth-century painting,</u> had been stolen from the museum. (The adjective clause modifies the subject, *The Winds of March.* There are two commas around this clause because it is in the middle of the sentence.)

Note: Do not use the word *that* with things if the adjective clause is nonessential. That is, don't use the word *that* immediately after a comma. In the above example, *which* is correct but *that* would be incorrect.

A. Find the adjective clause in each sentence below. Underline it and draw an arrow to the word(s) that it modifies.

1. Work, <u>which is a necessity for most of us,</u> is also enjoyable for many people.

2. The Puritans, who were among the earliest Europeans in North America, believed it was important to work hard.

3. The new immigrants worked to make a good life for their children, who had an easier life than that of their parents.

4. George, whose weekend had been full of activity, said he had been "relaxing."

5. She said she needed to get to class, which would begin in a few minutes.

B. Combine the following sentences. Make the second one of each pair into an adjective clause and add it to the first. Use commas. Follow the example.

1. He told her about *The Winds of March*.
   The Winds of March had been stolen.

   He told her about The Winds of March, which had been stolen.

2. Sharon had a business appointment.
   Sharon wasn't able to meet her friend until the next day.

   _____

   _____

3. He was the curator of the city art museum.
   The art museum had been robbed the day before.

   _____

   _____

4. Connie was going to be in town for two days.
   Connie's family had lived next to Sharon's family for many years.

   _____

   _____

5. The curator told her about Willie Brown.
   Willie Brown was a famous art thief.

   _____

   _____

6. Money was the motive for stealing the jewelry.
   The jewelry was very valuable.

   _____

   _____

7. The curator was proud of this work.
   The curator's museum was quite successful.

   _____

   _____

8. She waited anxiously for her secretary.
   Her secretary was at the library.

   _____

   _____

WRITING PARAGRAPHS: SUPPORTING MATERIAL (EXAMPLES)

As you saw in earlier chapters, a paragraph consists of a *topic sentence* with a number of *supporting sentences* about it. There are different kinds of supporting sentences; in Chapter 8, you learned that these may give *reasons*. Another kind of supporting sentence gives an *example* of information in the topic sentence. The paragraph may have several examples or just one.

Example:

Topic Sentence	People's attitudes (ideas) toward money often reflect cultural values. For
Supporting Material (Example 1)	example, most Americans wouldn't ask a friend how much money he makes or how much he paid for his new stereo. This reflects the American belief that privacy is very important. Another example is in borrowing
Supporting Material (Example 2)	and repaying money. If an American borrows money from a friend—even a small amount, such as a quarter or a dollar—he or she will almost always try to repay it. This reflects the American belief in the importance of independence. Americans don't like to feel dependent on others—or that they are taking something from them.

C.   On another piece of paper, write one paragraph about work and money in your country. Choose one of the following topics and write a topic sentence about it. Then write supporting sentences that are *examples*.

SUGGESTED TOPICS

attitudes toward money   borrowing money
a good kind of job   repaying money
making and keeping appointments   relaxation

10 Education

READING SKILLS:

Identifying the agent in the passive voice

Understanding newspaper headlines

WRITING SKILLS:

Using adjective clauses (review)

Writing paragraphs: supporting material (contrast)

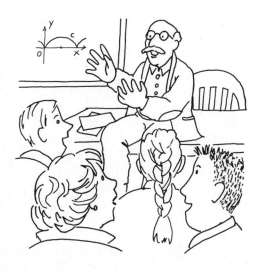

Part 1:   Fiction Reading

A. Picture clues. What do you think happens in Part 1 of the story? Before you read the story, look for clues in the pictures on this page. Then write T (true) or F (false) on the lines.

_____ 1. It seems to be a busy day at the Holmes Detective Agency.

_____ 2. Xenrovian scientists may have found something to help people who have cancer.

_____ 3. Something has happened in a place where scientists study and test drugs.

_____ 4. There has been a robbery.

_____ 5. The police and security guards know why the crime was committed.

B. Read the story. Try to guess the meaning of the new words. Don't use a dictionary.

The Crime on the Campus

It was a slow week at the Holmes Detective Agency. By Thursday morning Sharon and Elliot still didn't have any crimes to investigate. The phone hadn't rung even once all morning. Doris, the secretary, was rearranging the files. Sharon was reading the newspaper. Elliot, who was very bored, was making paper airplanes and aiming them at the wastepaper basket.

"Hmmm," said Sharon, pointing to a story on the front page of the paper. "Another article on this new anticancer drug from Xenrovia: 'Xenrovian Scientists Being Considered for Nobel Prize.'"

Just the day before, the headline of an article had read, "Big Step Against Cancer Taken in Xenrovia."

"Well, Uncle Sheerluck must be happy about *that*," Elliot said.

Sheerluck Holmes had immigrated from Xenrovia thirty years earlier. He was proud of his adopted country, where he was in charge of security at a local university, but he was also very proud of being Xenrovian and happy to hear of the success of Xenrovians.

Just as Sharon was reading the article out loud to Elliot and Doris, the office door opened. Sheerluck Holmes stepped in.

"My gosh," Elliot exclaimed, "this *is* a coincidence! Your name was just mentioned a minute ago."

Sharon put the paper down and smiled. "Have a seat, Uncle Sheerluck. Have you seen the article in today's paper?"

Sheerluck nodded.

"Isn't it wonderful news?"

Sheerluck hesitated. "Well, actually, it's not as good as it sounds," he said. "Turn to page four. There's another article there that you should read."

On page four, Sharon saw the article he was speaking of: "Formula Stolen from University Lab." Under this headline was a smaller headline: "Motive Unknown."

Elliot frowned slightly. "I don't understand. How is this article connected to the first one?"

Sheerluck Holmes sighed. "Some important papers and computer discs were stolen from a laboratory in our university medical center. Among those papers was the plan, the formula, for a new anticancer drug. The thief hasn't been found. I hate to say this, but I believe that a Xenrovian robbed the lab and sent the formula to Xenrovia."

"Oh, dear," said Sharon. "This is terrible."

"Yes," agreed Uncle Sheerluck. "But the worst part is this: the new drug was only being *tested*. It wasn't ready to be sold. Nobody knows for sure yet if it is safe. It could be very dangerous if the Xenrovians begin giving it to anyone who wants it."

"I see," said Elliot. "So you need to find the thief fast. Then you can persuade the Xenrovian government to refuse to permit the drug to be sold there. They'll need to wait until tests on it have been completed here."

"Exactly."

"How can we help?" asked Elliot.

"Well, I suspect that the thief is one of the professors at the medical center. Only eight people have keys to that laboratory, and five of them have been at the school for over twenty years. The other three are new. I believe that one of these three is Xenrovian. If so, this person is lying about his or her nationality; they all *claim* to be American. The person who is lying about this must be the thief. I'd like you and Sharon—and Doris—to help me find that person."

. . . To be continued

C. Did you understand the story? Answer these questions about it.

1. Why did Elliot expect Uncle Sheerluck to be happy?
2. What was Sheerluck Holmes' profession?
3. Where did Sheerluck Holmes think the Xenrovians had gotten the formula for the cancer drug?
4. Why might the new drug be dangerous?
5. How many people does Sheerluck want to investigate as possible criminals?
6. Who will probably help Sheerluck?

READING CLUE

The passive voice is often used *without* a phrase with *by*:

Example: They were surprised ~~by the news.~~

This is done because the agent (the person or thing after the word *by*) is (1) unknown, (2) not important to the meaning of the sentence, or (3) obvious or clear from the context. Or the agent may not be given because the writer wants to hide the information.

Example: Some information was stolen ~~by my friend.~~

D. What might be the missing agent in each of the following sentences? Look back at Part 1 of the story, if necessary, to find the context. Write *by* + agent (whom or what) on each line.

1. Your name was just mentioned a minute ago.

   (_____)

2. Some important papers and computer discs were recently stolen from a laboratory in our university medical center.

   (_____)

3. The thief hasn't been found. (_____)

4. The new drug was only being tested. (_____)

5. They'll need to wait until tests on it have been completed here.

   (_____)

READING CLUE

There are several special rules for understanding newspaper headlines. Some of these are:

1. Articles (*a, an, the*) are usually left out of headlines.
2. The passive voice is often used, but the verb *be* is missing.
3. When *be* is missing, the reader needs to imagine it there in either the simple present, simple past, or present perfect tense.
4. An infinitive in a headline usually means the future tense.

Examples: University Security Guards to Investigate Robbery
(= *The* university security guards *are going to* investigate *a* robbery.)
Detective Agency Asked to Help (= *A* detective agency *has been* asked to help.)

E. Decide which words are missing from these headlines. Then write the meaning of each headline. Use complete sentences.

1. Xenrovian Scientists Being Considered for Nobel Prize =

_____

_____

2. Big Step Against Cancer Taken in Xenrovia =

_____

3. Formula Stolen from University Lab =

_____

4. Motive Unknown =

_____

F. Read Part 1 of the story again and check your answers.

Part 2: Fiction Reading (continued)

A. Picture clues. What do you think happens in Part 2 of the story? Look for clues in the pictures. Then write T (true) or F (false) on the lines.

_____ 1. People who have cancer are going to Xenrovia for help.

_____ 2. Sheerluck Holmes is happy that cancer patients are going to Xenrovia.

_____ 3. The three professors probably don't know that detectives are sitting among their students.

_____ 4. Two professors seem to be very formal.

_____ 5. One professor seems to be friendly with his students.

B. Read the second part of the story. Think about the mystery.

The Crime on the Campus (continued)

"We'll do our best to help you find the thief," Elliot promised his uncle. "But what is your plan? Why have you come to us instead of your own security people on campus?"

"My security people would be easily recognized. I need people who aren't known in the university medical center. My plan is for you to spend time in classes. Pretend to be students. Try to find any clues you can to help me figure out if one of these people is Xenrovian. It won't be easy. None of them has a foreign accent, and they all *appear* to be American."

"But how was this person hired?" Sharon asked.

Sheerluck Holmes shrugged. "His—or her—papers were probably false. I'll be investigating this, but it might take time. I'm hoping that you can solve this mystery sooner than I can."

The four discussed the details of Sheerluck's plan and agreed to begin the next day.

"Then we'll meet back here on, say, Wednesday morning unless you learn something before then," Sheerluck said. "And . . . good luck."

In the next few days Elliot, Sharon, and Doris each attended the class of a different professor. They watched and listened carefully, took notes, talked with students at break time, and tried to find clues that might lead them to the Xenrovian thief.

During this time, there were several articles in the newspaper about the result of the robbery. The headline of one read: "New Xenrovian Drug Sought by Thousands of Cancer Patients." Another read: "Xenrovia Visited by Many Hopeful Cancer Patients." Each day the detectives became more worried. People were being given a drug that might be very dangerous.

On Wednesday morning, the detectives met again with Sheerluck Holmes.

"Unfortunately," Elliot said to his uncle, "I'm afraid we haven't found out much. As you said, each of the three professors *sounds* American and *acts* American. They're all very different from one another, of course, but as you know, this isn't strange. There is a wide variety of teaching styles in this country."

One by one, the detectives told about what they had noticed.

Elliot had attended a cardiology class. It was taught by Dr. Pauline Gray, a young woman who stood at a podium and gave serious, carefully prepared lectures. The students listened and took notes. They were permitted to ask questions during the last ten minutes of each class. They were expected to be on time for class and to do several hours of homework each night.

Sharon had attended a class called Priorities in Modern Health Care. It was taught in an informal style by an elderly man, Dr. Ralph Roman, who often didn't give a lecture at all. Instead, he frequently sat on his desk and involved the class in discussions. He and the students often laughed. Sometimes a student argued with another student or with the professor about the topic. Although the class was very relaxed, the students were expected to do a lot of homework and be prepared for the discussions. Also, they needed to write two long reports during the semester.

Doris had attended a course called Hospital Management. It was a formal class taught by Dr. Mark Smith. He was a very serious, well-organized, middle-aged man. Students were expected to be on time, to stand up when the professor entered, and to do a lot of homework. After class one day, Doris stayed to ask him a short question. He answered the question, and Doris smiled and thanked him. "I enjoy your class," she said, "but it's a little difficult for me. Maybe I'm too old to be a student again."

The professor nodded slightly and politely said, "Hmm. Well, I was quite surprised to see someone of your age in class. It's very unusual."

Sheerluck Holmes listened carefully to Elliot, Sharon, and Doris. Then he smiled.

The next day the headline of the university newspaper read: "Thief Arrested by Campus Security Chief." And two days after that the local newspaper carried an article that made the detectives especially relieved: "Cancer Drug Taken Off Market in Xenrovia; More Tests to Be Done."

With a little help, Sheerluck Holmes had solved the mystery.

C. Did you understand the story? Write G (for Dr. Pauline Gray, the first professor), R (for Dr. Ralph Roman, the second professor), or S (for Dr. Mark Smith, the third professor). In some cases, more than one answer is possible.

_____ 1. stood and spoke from a podium

_____ 2. didn't often give formal lectures

_____ 3. expected students to do a lot of homework

_____ 4. expected students to have a lot of class discussion

_____ 5. gently expressed surprise at having an older student in class

D. Can you figure it out? Answer these questions about the second half of the story. You'll get more information later.

1. Why did Sheerluck think that it would be difficult to figure out the identity of the Xenrovian thief?
2. In your opinion, is one of the styles of teaching in the story better than another? Which professor in the story is most similar to teachers in your country?
3. Did any of the professors do something that seemed strange to you? If so, what?

E. What might be the missing agent (*by whom or what*) in each of the following sentences? Look back at Part 2 of the story, if necessary, to find the context. Write *by* + agent (whom or what) on each line.

1. My security people would be easily recognized.

   (_____)

2. I need people who aren't known in the university medical center.

   (_____)

3. But how was this person hired?   (_____)

4. People were being given a drug that might be dangerous.

   (_____)

5. They were permitted to ask questions during the last ten minutes of

   each class.   (_____)

6. Students were expected to be on time, to stand up when the professor entered, and to do a lot of homework.

   (_____)

F. Decide which words are missing from these headlines. Then write the meaning of each headline. Use complete sentences.

1. New Xenrovian Drug Sought by Thousands of Cancer Patients =

   _____

   _____

2. Xenrovia Visited by Many Hopeful Cancer Patients =

   _____

   _____

3. Thief Arrested by Campus Security Chief =

   _____

4. Cancer Drug Taken Off Market in Xenrovia =

   _____

5. More Tests to Be Done =

   _____

G. Read Part 2 of the story again and check your answers.

Part 3: Nonfiction Reading

Understanding the American Educational System

In the American educational system, any student may attend a free public school from kindergarten (at about age five) through twelfth grade (about age eighteen). These public schools are all coeducational; that is, boys and girls study together in the same classes.

When students are in high school, they begin planning for college. Although many courses are required of all students, some courses are *electives*; they are chosen by students. For example, if a student wants to be prepared for college, he or she might choose to take chemistry, physics, an advanced mathematics class, or an advanced foreign language class. A student who doesn't plan to go to college might take auto mechanics, welding, or woodworking. After-school activities such as sports, drama, music, and student government are important to high school students.

Although there are no entrance exams for high school, there *is* an exam (called the S.A.T.—Scholastic Aptitude Test) that must be taken by students who want to go to a four-year college or university. However, colleges do not consider *only* this exam in deciding which students to accept. The students' grades in high school classes and participation in after-school activities are also extremely important.

At all levels of education in the United States, an important value is independence. Children in elementary school—as well as college and university students—are taught to think for themselves. They are taught that it is more important to be able to *find* an answer or to *figure it out* than simply to know it. For this reason, there is often a lot of discussion and independent research (careful study to find answers) in American education.

It is comparatively easy to enter an American college; however, it is *not* so easy to complete the coursework and graduate. Students need to study hard in college, and not everyone is able to finish.

Just as there is a great variety of courses at the college level, there is also a great variety of instructors. Many instructors give very formal classes. For example, they expect to be called by their title and last name ("*Professor* Adams," "*Ms.* Thompson," "*Mr.* Kramer"). They stand in front of the class and give formal lectures during which students take notes. Although they don't expect students to stand up when the instructor enters the room or when answering a question, they *do* appear to be very serious. Other instructors are informal; they prefer to be called by their first names. They might sit on the desk and expect students to participate in discussion with them. They try to make class enjoyable and sometimes joke with students. This informality, however, does not mean that they are not serious about teaching. They still expect students to study, do the homework, and do well on exams.

Cheating (using another student's answer on, for example, a quiz or test) is considered to be *very* improper, and it is taken seriously by all instructors. A student who has cheated on an exam will probably receive an "F" and might be dismissed from (kicked out of) school.

In the United States, people believe that "you're never too old to learn." For this reason, people of *any* age frequently take classes in a local adult school, community college, vocational school, or university extension program. People in their thirties, forties, fifties, and sixties may even decide to return to college on a part-time or full-time basis.

A. Can you solve the mystery? Study Part 2 of the story and answer these questions.

1. What did each professor expect of his or her students?
2. In what ways was Dr. Ralph Roman different from the other two professors?
3. What one thing did Dr. Mark Smith expect of his students that the other two didn't expect?
4. Why was Dr. Smith surprised to find Doris in his class?

B. Use the cultural information from this section to answer these questions.

1. Which professor did two things that are not done by American instructors in public colleges? What things did this person do?
2. Who was the Xenrovian thief? How do you know?

C. Discussing culture. Answer these questions. Try to use your new vocabulary words.

1. What do teachers in your country expect of their students? What do they *not* expect?
2. How are American teachers different from teachers in your country?
3. In your culture, do people in their thirties, forties, fifties, and sixties sometimes go back to school?
4. In what kind of classroom situation do you feel most comfortable— formal or informal? Why?

Part 4: Writing

A. Combine the following sentences. Make the second one of each pair into an adjective clause and decide where it belongs when you add it to the first. Then decide if you need to use commas or not. Follow the example.

1. Doris was rearranging the files.
   Doris didn't have anything else to do.

   Doris, who didn't have anything else to do, was rearranging the files.

2. Sharon was reading the newspaper.
   Sharon didn't like to sit and do nothing.

   _____

   _____

3. The newspaper article was about a new drug.
   She was reading the newspaper article.

   _____

   _____

4. He thought of his uncle.
   His uncle had immigrated thirty years earlier.
   (Note: He has only one uncle.)

   _____

   _____

5. They were trying to find the person.
   The person had stolen some papers and computer discs.

   _____

   _____

6. Dr. Gray's class was very difficult.
   Dr. Gray's class required hours of homework each night.

   _____

   _____

7. Dr. Roman believed that class discussion was important.
   Dr. Roman's teaching style was informal.

   _____

   _____

8. A person might have some difficulty in the beginning.
   A person is returning to school after many years.

   _____

   _____

9. All of his lectures were clear and easy to follow.
   All of his lectures had been carefully prepared.

_____

_____

WRITING PARAGRAPHS: SUPPORTING MATERIAL (CONTRAST)

In earlier chapters, you learned that supporting sentences in a paragraph may give *reasons* or *examples*. Another kind of supporting material shows *contrast*. There are two ways to organize sentences of contrast: A1, A2, A3, B1, B2, B3 or A1 B1, A2 B2, A3 B3.

Examples:

Although I enjoy both of my classes, my teachers are very different. One gives very formal classes. We call him by his last name (Mr. Brandreth). He gives interesting lectures, and we take notes. My other teacher gives very informal classes. She wants us to call her by her first name (Susana). She asks us a lot of questions, and she expects us to talk a lot.

Although I enjoy both of my classes, my teachers are very different. One teacher gives very formal classes. The other gives very informal classes. We call one by his last name (Mr. Brandreth). The other wants us to call her by her first name (Susana). Mr. Brandreth gives interesting lectures, and we take notes. Susana asks us a lot of questions, and she expects us to talk a lot.

B. On another piece of paper, write one paragraph about education. Choose one of the following topics and write a topic sentence about it. Then write supporting material of *contrast*.

    SUGGESTED TOPICS

    two classes (both in this country or one in your country and one here)

    two teachers

    public and private schools

    getting into college (in this country and your country)

    educational opportunities for older people (in this country and your country or in the past and the present)